# CSET General Science
## 215 Teacher Certification Exam

**By:** Sharon A. Wynne, M.S.

# XAMonline, INC.
Boston

Library of Congress Cataloging-in-Publication Data
Wynne, Sharon A.
    CSET General Science 215: Teacher Certification / Sharon A. Wynne.
    ISBN 978-1-64239-058-2
    1. General Science 215      2. Study Guides.      3. CSET
    4. Teachers' Certification & Licensure.    5. Careers

Managing Editor     Dr. Harte Weiner, Ph.D.
Copy Editor        Jeffrey Sack
Production Editor    David Aronson

**Disclaimer:**
The opinions expressed in this publication are the sole works of XAMonline and were created independently from the National Education Association, Educational Testing Service, or any State Department of Education, National Evaluation Systems or other testing affiliates.

Between the time of publication and printing, state specific standards as well as testing formats and website information may change that is not included in part or in whole within this product. Sample test questions are developed by XAMonline and reflect similar content as on real tests; however, they are not former tests. XAMonline assembles content that aligns with state standards but makes no claims nor guarantees teacher candidates a passing score. Numerical scores are determined by testing companies such as NES or ETS and then are compared with individual state standards. A passing score varies from state to state.

**Printed in the United States of America**        œ-1
CSET: General Science 215
ISBN: 978-1-64239-058-2

## *About the Subject Assessments*

## CSET™: Subject Assessment in the General Science Examination

**Purpose:** The assessments are designed to test the knowledge and competencies of prospective secondary level teachers. The question bank from which the assessment is drawn is undergoing constant revision. As a result, your test may include questions that will not count toward your score.

**Test Version:** There are two versions of subject assessment for General Science tests in California. General Science Subtest I (118) emphasizes comprehension in Astronomy, Dynamic Processes of Earth, Earth Resources, Waves, Forces and Motion, Electricity and Magnetism. General Science Subtest II (119) emphasizes comprehension in Ecology, Genetics and Evolution, Molecular Biology and Chemistry, Cell and Organismal Biology, Heat Transfer and Thermodynamics, Structures and Properties of Matter. Both exams are taken together in addition to one subtest either in Biology/Life Science, Chemistry, Physics or Earth and Planetary Science to receive the credential to teach general and integrated science in chosen subject areas. The General Science examination guide is based on a typical knowledge level of persons who have completed a *bachelor's degree program* in General Science.

**Time Allowance and Format:** You will have five hours to finish the test. Part of the test will consist of multiple-choice questions; part of the test will consist of focused and extended constructed-response questions. There are 116 multiple-choice questions and four focused constructed-response questions in the three subtests. If you pass one part of the exam, but not the other, you only need to retake the part you did not pass.

**Weighting:** There are seven multiple-choice questions in Subtest I in Astronomy; 15 multiple-choice questions and one focused constructed-response questions in the Dynamic Processes of Earth; seven multiple-choice questions in Earth Resources; eight multiple-choice questions in Waves; 15 multiple-choice questions and one focused constructed-response question in Forces and Motion; six multiple-choice questions in Electricity and Magnetism. There are eight multiple-choice questions in Subtest II in Ecology; 14 multiple-choice questions in Genetics and Evolution; seven multiple-choice questions and one focused constructed-response question in Molecular Biology and Chemistry; seven multiple-choice questions and one focused constructed-response question in Cell and Organismal Biology; seven multiple-choice questions in Heat Transfer and Thermodynamics; 15 multiple-choice questions in Structure and Properties of Matter.

**Additional Information about the CSET Assessments:** The CSET™ series subject assessments are developed *National Evaluation Systems.* They provide additional information on the CSET series assessments, including registration, preparation and testing procedures, study materials such as two topical guides, one for each subtest, that are all together about 59 pages of information including approximately 34 additional sample questions.

# Table of Contents

## Great Study and Testing Tips!

*What* to study in order to prepare for the subject assessments is the focus of this study guide but equally important is *how* you study.

You can increase your chances of truly mastering the information by taking some simple, but effective steps.

## Study Tips:

**1. <u>Some foods aid the learning process</u>.** Foods such as milk, nuts, seeds, rice, and oats help your study efforts by releasing natural memory enhancers called CCKs (*cholecystokinin*) composed of *tryptophan*, *choline*, and *phenylalanine*. All of these chemicals enhance the neurotransmitters associated with memory. Before studying, try a light, protein-rich meal of eggs, turkey, and fish. All of these foods release the memory enhancing chemicals. The better the connections, the more you comprehend.

Likewise, before you take a test, stick to a light snack of energy boosting and relaxing foods. A glass of milk, a piece of fruit, or some peanuts all release various memory-boosting chemicals and help you to relax and focus on the subject at hand.

**2. <u>Learn to take great notes</u>.** A by-product of our modern culture is that we have grown accustomed to getting our information in short doses (i.e. TV news sound bites or USA Today style newspaper articles.)

Consequently, we've subconsciously trained ourselves to assimilate information better in <u>neat little packages</u>. If your notes are scrawled all over the paper, it fragments the flow of the information. Strive for clarity. Newspapers use a standard format to achieve clarity. Your notes can be much clearer through use of proper formatting. A very effective format is called the *<u>"Cornell Method."</u>*

Take a sheet of loose-leaf lined notebook paper and draw a line all the way down the paper about 1-2" from the left-hand edge.

Draw another line across the width of the paper about 1-2" up from the bottom. Repeat this process on the reverse side of the page.

Look at the highly effective result. You have ample room for notes, a left hand margin for special emphasis items or inserting supplementary data from the textbook, a large area at the bottom for a brief summary, and a little rectangular space for just about anything you want.

**3. Get the concept then the details.** Too often we focus on the details and don't gather an understanding of the concept. However, if you simply memorize only dates, places, or names, you may well miss the whole point of the subject.

A key way to understand things is to put them in your own words. If you are working from a textbook, automatically summarize each paragraph in your mind. If you are outlining text, don't simply copy the author's words.

*Rephrase* them in your own words. You remember your own thoughts and words much better than someone else's, and subconsciously tend to associate the important details to the core concepts.

**4. Ask Why?** Pull apart written material paragraph by paragraph and don't forget the captions under the illustrations.

Example: If the heading is "Stream Erosion", flip it around to read, "Why do streams erode?" Then answer the questions.

If you train your mind to think in a series of questions and answers, not only will you learn more, but it also helps to lessen the test anxiety because you are used to answering questions.

**5. Read for reinforcement and future needs.** Even if you only have 10 minutes, put your notes or a book in your hand. Your mind is similar to a computer; you have to input data in order to have it processed. *By reading, you are creating the neural connections for future retrieval.* The more times you read something, the more you reinforce the learning of ideas.

Even if you don't fully understand something on the first pass, *your mind stores much of the material for later recall.*

**6. Relax to learn so go into exile.** Our bodies respond to an inner clock called biorhythms. Burning the midnight oil works well for some people, but not everyone. If possible, set aside a particular place to study that is free of distractions. Shut off the television, cell phone, and pager and exile your friends and family during your study period.

If you really are bothered by silence, try background music. Light classical music at a low volume has been shown to aid in concentration over other types. Music that evokes pleasant emotions without lyrics is highly suggested. Try just about anything by Mozart. It relaxes you.

**7. Use arrows not highlighters.** At best, it's difficult to read a page full of yellow, pink, blue, and green streaks. Try staring at a neon sign for a while and you'll soon see that the horde of colors obscure the message.

A quick note, a brief dash of color, an underline, and an arrow pointing to a particular passage is much clearer than a horde of highlighted words.

**8. Budget your study time.** Although you shouldn't ignore any of the material, *allocate your available study time in the same ratio that topics may appear on the test.*

## Testing Tips:

**1. Get smart, play dumb. Don't read anything into the question.** Don't make an assumption that the test writer is looking for something else than what is asked. Stick to the question as written and don't read extra things into it.

**2. Read the question and all the choices *twice* before answering the question.** You may miss something by not carefully reading, and then re-reading both the question and the answers.

If you really don't have a clue as to the right answer, leave it blank on the first time through. Go on to the other questions, as they may provide a clue as to how to answer the skipped questions.

If later on, you still can't answer the skipped ones . . . *Guess.* The only penalty for guessing is that you *might* get it wrong. Only one thing is certain; if you don't put anything down, you will get it wrong!

**3. Turn the question into a statement.** Look at the way the questions are worded. The syntax of the question usually provides a clue. Does it seem more familiar as a statement rather than as a question? Does it sound strange?

By turning a question into a statement, you may be able to spot if an answer sounds right, and it may also trigger memories of material you have read.

**4. Look for hidden clues.** It's actually very difficult to compose multiple-foil (choice) questions without giving away part of the answer in the options presented.

In most multiple-choice questions you can often readily eliminate one or two of the potential answers. This leaves you with only two real possibilities and automatically your odds go to fifty-fifty for very little work.

**5. Trust your instincts.** For every fact that you have read, you subconsciously retain something of that knowledge. On questions that you aren't really certain about, go with your basic instincts. **Your first impression on how to answer a question is usually correct.**

6. <u>**Mark your answers directly on the test booklet.**</u> Don't bother trying to fill in the optical scan sheet on the first pass through the test. *Just be very careful not to miss-mark your answers when you eventually transcribe them to the scan sheet.*

7. <u>**Watch the clock**</u>! You have a set amount of time to answer the questions. Don't get bogged down trying to answer a single question at the expense of 10 questions you can more readily answer.

COMPETENCY 1.0        KNOWLEDGE OF SCIENTIFIC PROCESSES AND
                      THE LABORATORY

SKILL 1.1    Apply knowledge of the primary processes of science:
             observing, inferring, measuring (metric system),
             communicating/graphing, and classifying.

Science may be defined as a body of knowledge that is systematically derived
from study, observations and experimentation. Its goal is to identify and establish
principles and theories that may be applied to solve problems. Pseudoscience,
on the other hand, is a belief that is not warranted. There is no scientific
methodology or application. Some of the more classic examples of
pseudoscience include witchcraft, alien encounters, or any topics that are
explained by hearsay.

Science uses the metric system as it is accepted worldwide and allows easier
comparison among experiments done by scientists around the world. Learn the
following basic units and prefixes:

> **meter** - measure of length
> **liter** - measure of volume
> **gram** - measure of mass

**deca**-(meter, liter, gram)= 10X the base unit    **deci** = 1/10 the base unit
**hecto**-(meter, liter, gram)= 100X the base unit  **centi** = 1/100 the base unit
**kilo**-(meter, liter, gram)  = 1000X the base unit **milli** = 1/1000 the base unit

**Graphing** is an important skill to visually display collected data for analysis. The
two types of graphs most commonly used are the **line graph** and the **bar graph**
(histogram). Line graphs are set up to show two variables represented by one
point on the graph. The X-axis is the horizontal axis and represents the
independent variable. Independent variables are those that would be changed by
the experimenter. A common example of an independent variable is time. Time
proceeds regardless of anything else going on. The Y-axis is the vertical axis and
represents the dependent variable. Dependent variables are observed to see
how they are affected by the change to the independent variable. An example of
a dependent variable would be the growth or the height of a plant. Graphs should
be calibrated at equal intervals. If one space represents one day, the next space
may not represent 10 days. A "best fit" line is drawn to join the points and may
not include all the points in the data. Axes must always be labeled or the graph
means nothing. A good title will describe both the dependent and the
independent variables. Bar graphs are set up similarly in regards to axes, but
points are not plotted. Instead, the dependent variable is set up as a bar where
the X-axis intersects with the Y-axis. Each bar is a separate item of data and is
not joined by a continuous line.

**Classifying** is grouping items according to their similarities. It is important for students to realize relationships and similarity as well as differences to reach a reasonable conclusion in a lab experience.

**SKILL 1.2** **Apply knowledge of the integrated processes of science: forming hypothesis, manipulating variables (manipulated, responding, held constant), defining operationally, interpreting data, and using indirect evidence and models.**

The scientific method is the basic process behind science. It involves several steps from formulating a hypothesis to deriving the conclusion.

**Posing a question**
Although many discoveries happen by chance, the standard thought process of a scientist begins with forming a question to research. The more limited the question, the easier it is to set up an experiment to answer it.

**Forming a hypothesis**
Once the question is formulated, take an educated guess about the answer to the problem or question.

**Doing the test**
To make a test fair, data from an experiment must have a **variable** or any condition that can be changed—such as temperature or mass. A good test will try to manipulate as few variables as possible to see which variable is responsible for the result. This requires a second example of a **control**. A control is an extra setup in which all the conditions are the same except for the variable being tested.

**Observing and recording the data**
When reporting data, students should be taught to specify how they calculated the measurements. They should also know the proper procedures for reading a graduated cylinder. Teaching proper technique is a critical part of the instructional process so that students may attribute validity to their data.

**Drawing a conclusion**
After you take your data, you compare it to the other groups of data. A conclusion is the judgment derived from the results.

**Graphing data**
Graphing takes numbers and shows patterns that might otherwise be difficult from which to make conclusions.

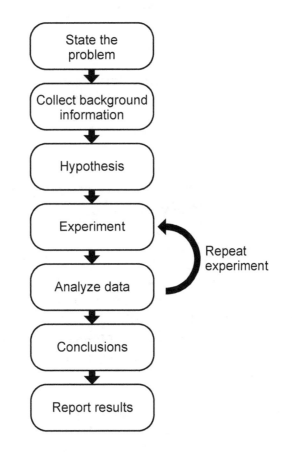

## SKILL 1.3    Apply knowledge of designing and performing investigations.

Normally, knowledge is integrated in the form of a laboratory report. It should include a specific title and tell exactly what is being studied. At the very top of the report is an **abstract**—a summary of the report. It defines the purpose and states the problem being tested. The purpose should include the **hypothesis** (educated guess) of what is expected from the outcome of the experiment. The entire experiment should relate to this problem. It is important to describe exactly what was done to support or disprove a hypothesis. A **control** is necessary to show that the results occurred from the changed conditions and would not just happen normally. Only one variable should be manipulated at one time. **Observations** and results of the experiment should be recorded, including all results from data. Drawings, graphs and illustrations should be included to support the information. Observations are objective, whereas analysis and interpretation is subjective. A **conclusion** should explain why the results of the experiment either supported or disproved the hypothesis.

A scientific theory is an explanation of a set of related observations based on a proven hypothesis. A scientific law usually lasts longer than a scientific theory and has more data to back it up.

### SKILL 1.4  Perform basic science calculations (e.g. molar, percent solutions, proportions and rates).

**Moles** = mass X 1 mole/molecular weight

Example: Determine the moles of 20 grams of water. To solve this, take the water's mass (20 g) and multiply it by 1 mole of water, and then divide it by the molecular weight of a molecule of water (18 g).

20g X 1mole /18g= 1.11 moles

**Percent solution** and **proportions** are basically the same thing. To find percent volume, divide the grams of the substance by the amount of the solvent. For example, 20 grams of salt divided by 100 ml of water would result in a 20% solution of saltwater. To determine percent mass, divide the ml of substance being mixed by the amount of solvent. Percent mass is not used as often as percent volume.

**Rate** is determined by dividing the change in distance (or the independent variable) by the change in time. If a plant grew four centimeters in two days, the rate of growth would be two centimeters per day.

### SKILL 1.5  Identify procedures for proper use, care and handling of laboratory animals, plants and protists.

**Dissections** - Animals not obtained from recognized sources should not be used. Decaying animals or those of unknown origin may harbor pathogens and/or parasites. Specimens should be rinsed before handling. Latex gloves are desirable. If gloves are not available, students with sores or scratches should be excused from the activity. While not used as often, some specimens may be preserved in a chemical called formaldehyde. Formaldehyde is a carcinogen (causes cancer) and should be avoided or disposed of according to district regulations. Most specimens from reputable supply houses are preserved in karosafe or bioguard. Both of these chemicals, while aromatic, are not dangerous. Students objecting to dissections for moral reasons should be given an alternative assignment.

**Live specimens** - No dissections may be performed on living mammalian vertebrates or birds. Lower-order life and invertebrates may be used, if school policy allows. Biological experiments may be done with all animals except mammalian vertebrates or birds. No physiological harm may result to the animal. All animals housed and cared for in the school must be handled in a safe and humane manner. Animals are not to remain on school premises during extended vacations unless adequate care is provided. Many state laws state that any instructor who intentionally refuses to comply with the laws may be suspended or dismissed.

**Microbiology** - Pathogenic organisms must never be used for experimentation. Students should adhere to the following rules at all times when working with microorganisms to avoid accidental contamination:

1. Treat all microorganisms as if they were pathogenic.
2. Maintain sterile conditions at all times.

If you are taking a national level exam, you should check with the Department of Education for your state for safety procedures. You will want to know what your state expects of you not only for the test but also for performance in the classroom for the welfare of your students and others.

**SKILL 1.6    Identify the laboratory equipment to be used for specific activities (e.g. voltmeter, volumetric flask, hygrometer, microscope and balance).**

**Bunsen burners** - Hot plates should be used whenever possible to avoid the risk of burns or fire. If Bunsen burners are used, the following precautions should be followed:

1. Know the location of fire extinguishers and safety blankets and train students in their use. Long hair and long sleeves should be secured and out of the way.

2. Turn the gas on all the way and make a spark with the striker.

3. Adjust the air valve at the bottom of the Bunsen burner until the flame shows an inner cone.

4. Adjust the flow of gas to the desired flame height by using the adjustment valve.

5. Do not touch the barrel of the burner, as it is hot.

6. The preferred method to light burners is to use a striker rather than a match.

**Graduated Cylinder** - These are used for precise measurements. They should always be placed on a flat surface. The surface of the liquid will form a meniscus (a lens-shaped curve). The measurement is read at the bottom of this curve.

**Balance** - Electronic balances are easier to use, but more expensive. An electronic balance should always be zeroed out before measuring and used on a flat surface. Substances should always be placed on a piece of paper to avoid messes and damage to the instrument. Triple beam balances must be used on a level surface. There are screws located at the bottom of the balance to make any adjustments. Start with the largest counterweight first to the last notch that does not tip the balance. Do the same with the next largest, etc., until the pointer levels at zero. The total mass is the total of all the readings on the beams. Again, use paper under the substance to protect the equipment.

**Burette** – A burette is used to dispense precisely measured volumes of liquid. A stopcock is used to control the volume of liquid being dispensed at a time.

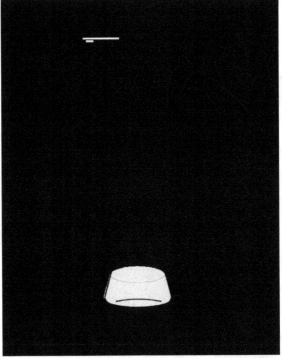

Light microscopes are commonly used in laboratory experiments. Several procedures should be followed to properly care for this equipment:

- Clean all lenses with lens paper only.
- Carry microscopes with two hands; one on the arm and one on the base.
- Always begin focusing on low power, then switch to high power.
- Store microscopes with the low power objective down.
- Always use a coverslip when viewing wet mount slides.
- Bring the objective down to its lowest position then focus moving up to avoid breaking the slide or scratching the lens.

Wet mount slides should be made by placing a drop of water on the specimen and then putting a glass coverslip on top of the drop of water. Dropping the coverslip at a 45 degree angle will help in avoiding air bubbles. Total magnification is determined by multiplying the ocular (usually 10X) and the objective (usually 10X on low, 40X on high).

### SKILL 1.7  Identify sources of laboratory materials and adequate Substitutions.

Laboratory materials are readily available from the many school suppliers that routinely send their catalogs to schools. Many times, common materials are available at the local grocery store. The use of locally available flora and fauna both reduces the cost and familiarizes students with the organisms where they live. Innovation and networking with other science teachers will assist in keeping costs of lab materials to a minimum.

### SKILL 1.8  Identify state laws or regulations related to teaching Science.

All science labs should contain the following items of safety equipment. The following are required by law.

- Fire blanket which is visible and accessible
- Ground Fault Circuit Interrupters (GCFI) within two feet of water supplies.
- Signs designating emergency exits
- Emergency shower providing a continuous flow of water
- Emergency eye wash station that can be activated by the foot or forearm
- Eye protection for every student and a means of sanitizing equipment
- Emergency exhaust fans providing ventilation to the outside of the building.
- Master cut-off switches for gas, electric and compressed air. Switches must have permanently attached handles. Cut-off switches must be clearly labeled.
- An ABC fire extinguisher
- Storage cabinets for flammable materials

*Also recommended, but not required by law:*
- Chemical spill control kit
- Fume hood with a motor that is spark proof
- Protective laboratory aprons made of flame retardant material
- Signs which will alert potential hazardous conditions
- Containers for broken glassware, flammables, corrosives and waste
- Containers should be labeled

It is the responsibility of teachers to provide a safe environment for their students. Proper supervision greatly reduces the risk of injury; a teacher should never leave a class for any reason without providing alternate supervision. After an accident, two factors are considered: foreseeability and negligence. **Foreseeability** is the anticipation that an event may occur under certain circumstances. **Negligence** is the failure to exercise ordinary or reasonable care. Safety procedures should be a part of the science curriculum; a well-managed classroom is important to avoid potential lawsuits.

The **Hazard Communication "Right to Know" regulation** covers science teachers who work with potentially hazardous chemicals. Briefly, the law states that employees must be informed of potentially toxic chemicals. An inventory must be made available if requested. The inventory must contain information about the hazards and properties of the chemicals. Training must be provided in the safe handling and interpretation of the Safety Data Sheet (SDS). Every chemical that is available on site must be accompanied by a Safety Data Sheet.

The following chemicals are potential carcinogens and not allowed in school facilities:

> Acrylonitrile, Arsenic compounds, Asbestos, Benzidine, Benzene, Cadmium compounds, Chloroform, Chromium compounds, Ethylene oxide, Ortho-toluidine, Nickel powder, Mercury.

### SKILL 1.9 Identify the accepted procedures for safe use, storage, and disposal of chemicals.

All laboratory solutions should be prepared as directed in the laboratory manual. Care should be taken to avoid contamination. All glassware should be triple-rinsed with distilled water before using, and cleaned well after use. Safety goggles should be worn while working with glassware in case of an accident. All solutions should be made with distilled water as tap water contains dissolved particles that may affect the results of an experiment. Chemical storage should be located in a secured, dry area. Chemicals should be stored in accordance with what they react. Acids are to be locked in a separate area. Used solutions should be disposed of according to local disposal procedures. Any questions regarding safe disposal or chemical safety may be directed to the local fire department.

## SKILL 1.10 Identify current technologies and its uses in the sciences (e.g. computerization, satellites, sonar, seismographic instrumentation, medicine, agriculture and spectrometry).

**Chromatography** uses the principles of capillarity to separate substances such as plant pigments. Molecules of a larger size will move slower up the paper, whereas smaller molecules will move more quickly producing lines of pigments.

**Spectrophotometry** uses percent light absorbance to measure a color change, thus giving qualitative data a quantitative value.

**Centrifugation** involves spinning substances at a high speed. The denser portion of a solution will settle to the bottom of the test tube; whereas the lighter materials will stay on top. Centrifugation is used to separate blood into blood cells and plasma, with heavier blood cells settling to the bottom.

**Electrophoresis** uses electrical charges of molecules to separate them according to their size. The molecules, such as DNA or proteins, are pulled through a gel toward either the positive end of the gel box (if the material has a negative charge) or the negative end of the gel box (if the material has a positive charge).

**Computer technology** has greatly improved the collection and interpretation of scientific data. Molecular findings have been enhanced through the use of computer images. Technology has revolutionized access to data via the Internet and shared databases, and sophisticated software programs now allow better manipulation of data. Advances in computer engineering have produced MRI's, CT scans, and other devices in medicine and laser technology, allowing numerous applications and refined precision.

**Satellites** have improved our ability to communicate and transmit radio and television signals. Navigational abilities have been greatly improved through the use of satellite signals. Sonar uses sound waves to locate objects, primarily underwater. Sound waves bounce off objects and are picked up to assist in location. Seismographs record vibrations in the earth and allow us to measure earthquake activity.

## COMPETENCY 2.0      KNOWLEDGE OF CHEMISTRY

### SKILL 2.1    Identify the physical and chemical properties of matter (e.g. mass, weight, volume, identity, and reactivity).

Everything in our world is made up of **matter**, whether it is a rock, a building, an animal, or a person. Matter is defined by its characteristics: It takes up space and has mass.

**Mass** is a measure of the amount of matter in an object. Two objects of equal mass will balance each other on a simple balance scale no matter where the scale is located. For instance, two rocks with the same amount of mass that are in balance on Earth will also be in balance on the moon. They will feel heavier on Earth than on the moon because of Earth's gravitational pull. So, although the two rocks have the same mass, they will have different **weights.**

**Weight** is the measure of Earth's pull of gravity on an object. It can also be defined as the pull of gravity between other bodies. The unit of weight measure commonly used is the pound in English and the kilogram in metric measurements.

In addition to mass, matter also has the property of volume. **Volume** is the amount of space that an object occupies. Volume and mass together give a more exact description of the object. Two objects may have the same volume, but different mass, the same mass but different volumes, etc. For instance, consider two cubes that are each one cubic centimeter, one made from plastic, and one from lead. They have the same volume, but the lead cube has more mass. The measure that we use to describe the cubes takes into consideration both the mass and the volume. **Density** is the mass of a substance contained per unit of volume. If the density of an object is less than the density of a liquid, the object will float in the liquid. If the object is denser than the liquid, then the object will sink.

Density is stated in grams per cubic centimeter ($g / cm^3$) where the gram is the standard unit of mass. To find an object's density, you must measure its mass and its volume. Then divide the mass by the volume ($D = m / V$).

To find an object's density, first use a balance to find its mass. Then calculate its volume. If the object is regular shape, like a cube, you can find the volume by multiplying the length, width, and height together. However, if it is an irregular shape, you can find the volume by seeing how much water it displaces. Measure the water in the container before and after the object is submerged. The difference will be the volume of the object.

**Specific gravity** is the ratio of the density of a substance to the density of water. For instance, the specific density of one liter of turpentine is calculated by comparing its mass (0.81 kg) to the mass of one liter of water (1 kg):

$$\frac{\text{mass of 1 L alcohol}}{\text{mass of 1 L water}} = \frac{0.81 \text{ kg}}{1.00 \text{ kg}} = 0.81$$

Physical properties and chemical properties of matter describe the appearance or behavior of a substance. **Physical properties** are observed without changing the identity of a substance. For instance, you can describe the color, mass, shape, and volume of a book. **Chemical properties** describe the ability of a substance to be changed into new substances. Baking powder goes through a chemical change as it changes into carbon dioxide gas during the baking process.

Matter constantly changes. A **physical change** is a change that does not produce a new substance. The freezing and melting of water is an example of physical change. A **chemical change (or chemical reaction)** is any change of a substance into one or more other substances. Burning materials turn into smoke; a seltzer tablet fizzes into gas bubbles.

### SKILL 2.2 Distinguish among solids, liquids, and gases

The **phase of matter** (solid, liquid, or gas) is identified by its shape and volume. A **solid** has a definite shape and volume. A **liquid** has a definite volume, but no shape. A **gas** has no shape or volume because it will spread out to occupy the entire space of its container.

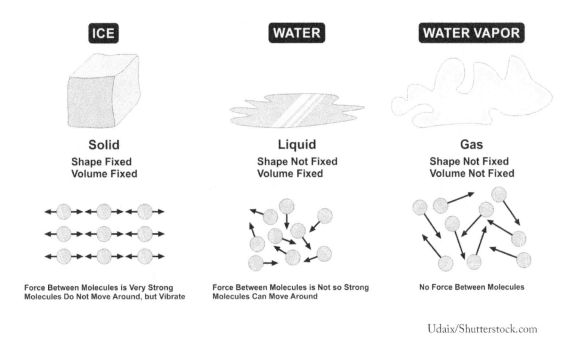

| ICE | WATER | WATER VAPOR |
|:---:|:---:|:---:|
| Solid | Liquid | Gas |
| Shape Fixed<br>Volume Fixed | Shape Not Fixed<br>Volume Fixed | Shape Not Fixed<br>Volume Not Fixed |
| Force Between Molecules is Very Strong<br>Molecules Do Not Move Around, but Vibrate | Force Between Molecules is Not so Strong<br>Molecules Can Move Around | No Force Between Molecules |

Udaix/Shutterstock.com

**Energy** is the ability to cause change in matter. Applying heat to a frozen liquid changes it from solid back to liquid. Continue heating it and it will boil and give off steam, a gas.

**Evaporation** is the change in phase from liquid to gas. **Condensation** is the change in phase from gas to liquid.

### SKILL 2.3    Apply knowledge of the gas laws (e.g. relationships among temperature, pressure, and volume of gases).

As a substance is heated, the molecules begin moving faster within the container. As the substance becomes a gas and those molecules hit the sides of the container, pressure builds. **Pressure** is the force exerted on each unit of area of a surface. Pressure is measured in a unit called the **Pascal**. One Pascal (pa) is equal to one Newton of force pushing on one square meter of area.

Volume, temperature, and pressure of gas are related.

**Temperature and pressure:** As the temperature of a gas increases, its pressure increases. When you drive a car, the friction between the road and the tire heats up the air inside the tire. Because the temperature increases, so does the pressure of the air on the inside of the tire.

**Temperature and Volume:** At a constant pressure, an increase in temperature causes an increase in the volume of a gas. If you apply heat to an enclosed container of gas, the pressure inside the bottle will increase as the heat increases. This is called **Charles' Law**.

These relations (pressure and temperature, and temperature and volume) are **direct variations**. As one component increases (decreases), the other also increases (decreases).

However, pressure and volume vary inversely.

**Pressure and volume:** At a constant temperature, a decrease in the volume of a gas causes an increase in its pressure. An example of this is a tire pump. The gas pressure inside the pump gets bigger as you press down on the pump handle because you are compressing the gas, or forcing it to exist in a smaller volume. This relationship between pressure and volume is called **Boyle's Law**.

### SKILL 2.4    Identify the characteristics of elements, compounds, and mixtures

An **element** is a substance that cannot be broken down into other substances. The most recent publications report that scientists have identified 118 elements: 94 are found in nature and 24 are synthetic.

An **atom** is the smallest particle of the element that has the properties of that element. All of the atoms of a particular element are the same. The atoms of each element are different from the atoms of the other elements.

Elements are assigned an identifying symbol of one or two letters. The symbol for oxygen is O and stands for one atom of oxygen. However, because oxygen atoms in nature are joined together in pairs, the symbol $O_2$ represents oxygen. This pair of oxygen molecules is a molecule. A **molecule** is the smallest particle of substance that can exist independently and has all of the properties of that substance. A molecule of most elements is made up of one atom. However, oxygen, hydrogen, nitrogen, and chlorine molecules are made of two atoms each.

A **compound** is made of two or more elements that have been chemically combined. Atoms join together when elements are chemically combined. The result is that the elements lose their individual identities when they are joined. The compound that they become has different properties.

We use a formula to show the elements of a chemical compound. A **chemical formula** is a shorthand way of showing what is in a compound by using symbols and subscripts. The letter symbols let us know what elements are involved and the number subscript tells how many atoms of each element are involved. No subscript is used if there is only one atom involved. For example, carbon dioxide is made up of one atom of carbon (C) and two atoms of oxygen ($O_2$), so the formula would be represented as: $CO_2$.

Substances can combine without a chemical change. A **mixture** is any combination of two or more substances in which the substances keep their own properties. A fruit salad is a mixture. So is an ice cream sundae, although you might not recognize each part if it is stirred together. Colognes and perfumes are other examples. You may not readily recognize the individual elements. However, they can be separated.

**Compounds** and **mixtures** are similar in that they are made up of two or more substances. However, they have the following opposite characteristics:

### Compounds:
1. Made up of one kind of particle
2. Formed during a chemical change
3. Broken down only by chemical changes
4. Properties are different from its parts
5. Has a specific amount of each ingredient

### Mixtures:
1. Made up of two or more particles
2. Not formed by a chemical change
3. Can be separated by physical changes
4. Properties are the same as its parts
5. Does not have a definite amount of each ingredient

Common compounds are **acids, bases, salts**, and **oxides** and are classified according to their characteristics.

An **acid** contains hydrogen ions (H+). Although it is never wise to taste a substance to identify it, acids have a sour taste. Vinegar and lemon juice are both acids, and acids occur in many foods in a weak state. Strong acids can burn skin and destroy materials. Common acids include:

| | | |
|---|---|---|
| Sulfuric acid ($H_2SO_4$) | - | Used in medicines, alcohol, dyes, and car batteries |
| Nitric acid ($HNO_3$) | - | Used in fertilizers, explosives, cleaning materials |
| Carbonic acid ($H_2CO_3$) | - | Used in soft drinks |
| Acetic acid ($HC_2H_3O_2$) | - | Used in making plastics, rubber, photographic film, and as a solvent |

**Bases** have a bitter taste and the stronger ones feel slippery. Like acids, strong bases can be dangerous and should be handled carefully. All bases contain hydroxyl ions (OH-). Many household cleaning products contain bases. Common bases include:

| | | | |
|---|---|---|---|
| Sodium hydroxide | (NaOH) | - | Used in making soap, paper, vegetable oils, and refining petroleum |
| Ammonium hydroxide | (NH$_4$OH) | - | Making deodorants, bleaching compounds, cleaning compounds |
| Potassium hydroxide | (KOH) | - | Making soaps, drugs, dyes, alkaline batteries, and purifying industrial gases |
| Calcium hydroxide | (Ca(OH)$_2$) | - | Making cement and plaster |

An **indicator** is a substance that changes color when it comes in contact with an acid or a base. Litmus paper is an indicator. Blue litmus paper turns red in an acid. Red litmus paper turns blue in a base.

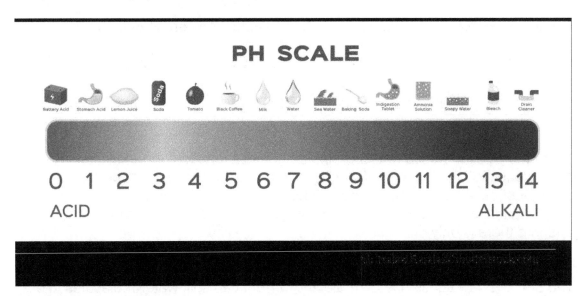

A substance that is neither acid nor base is **neutral**. Neutral substances do not change the color of litmus paper.

**Salt** is formed when an acid and a base combine chemically. Water is also formed. The process is called **neutralization**. Table salt (NaCl) is an example of this process. Salts are also used in toothpaste, Epsom salts, and cream of tartar. Calcium chloride (CaCl$_2$) is used on frozen streets and walkways to melt the ice.

**Oxides** are compounds that are formed when oxygen combines with another element. Rust is an oxide formed when oxygen combines with iron.

### SKILL 2.5     Apply knowledge of symbols, formulas, and equations related to common elements and compounds and their reactions.

One or more substances are formed during a **chemical reaction**. Also, energy is released during some chemical reactions. Sometimes the energy release is slow and sometimes it is rapid. In a fireworks display, energy is released very rapidly. However, the chemical reaction that produces tarnish on a silver spoon happens very slowly.

Chemical equilibrium is defined as when the quantities of reactants and products are at a 'steady state' and no longer shifting, but the reaction may still proceed forward and backward. The rate of forward reaction must equal the rate of backward reaction.

For more information on chemical reactions, also see section 2.11: Identify types of chemical reactions and their characteristics.

In one kind of chemical reaction, two elements combine to form a new substance. We can represent the reaction and the results in a chemical equation.

Carbon and oxygen form carbon dioxide. The equation can be written:

$$C \quad + \quad O_2 \quad \rightarrow \quad CO_2$$

| 1 atom of carbon | + | 1 atom of oxygen | → | 1 molecule of carbon dioxide |
|---|---|---|---|---|

No matter is ever gained or lost during a chemical reaction; therefore, the chemical equation must be *balanced.* This means that there must be the same number of molecules on both sides of the equation. Remember that the subscript numbers indicate the number of atoms in the elements. If there is no subscript, assume there is only one atom.

In a second kind of chemical reaction, the molecules of a substance split, forming two or more new substances. An electric current can split water molecules into hydrogen and oxygen gas.

$$2H_2O \quad \rightarrow \quad 2H_2 \quad - \quad O_2$$

| 2 molecules of water | → | 2 molecules of hydrogen | - | 1 molecule of oxygen |
|---|---|---|---|---|

The number of molecules is shown by the number in front of an element or compound. If no number appears, assume that it is 1 molecule.

A third kind of chemical reaction is when elements change places with each other. An example of one element taking the place of another is when iron changes places with copper in the compound copper sulfate:

| $CuSo_4$ | + | Fe | $\rightarrow$ | $FeSO_4$+ | Cu |
|---|---|---|---|---|---|
| copper | + | iron | | iron | copper |
| sulfate | | (steel wool) | | sulfate | |

Sometimes two sets of elements change places. In this example, an acid and a base are combined:

| HCl | + | NaOH | $\rightarrow$ | NaCl | + | $H_2O$ |
|---|---|---|---|---|---|---|
| hydrochloric acid | | sodium hydroxide | | sodium chloride (table salt) | | water |

Matter can change, but it cannot be created or destroyed. The sample equations show two things:

1. In a chemical reaction, matter is changed into one or more different kinds of matter.
2. The amount of matter present before and after the chemical reaction is the same.

Many chemical reactions give off energy. Like matter, energy can change form, but it can neither be created nor destroyed during a chemical reaction. This is the **law of conservation of energy.**

### SKILL 2.6    Identify the major events in the development of the atomic theory.

The **atomic theory of matter** suggests that:

1. All matter consists of atoms
2. All atoms of an element are identical
3. Different elements have different atoms
4. Atoms maintain their properties in a chemical reaction

The atomic theory of matter was first suggested by a Greek named **Democritus.** The atomic theory of matter states that matter is made up of tiny, rapidly moving particles. These particles move more quickly when warmer, because temperature is a measure of average kinetic energy of the particles. Warmer molecules therefore move further away from each other, with enough energy to separate from each other more often and for greater distances.

Much later (1780's), a scientist named **John Dalton** expanded on Democritus' idea. Dalton, a schoolteacher, made some observations about air: air is a mixture of different kinds of gases; these gases do not separate on their own; it is possible to compress gases into a smaller volume. He also thought that particles of different substances must be different from each other and must maintain their own mass when combined with other substances.

**Dalton's Model of the Atom:**

1. Matter is made up of atoms.
2. Atoms of an element are similar to each other.
3. Atoms of different elements are different from each other.
4. Atoms combine with each other to form new kinds of compounds.

The present model of the atom is much different from Dalton's model.

In the late 1800's, a British scientist named J.J. **Thompson** was studying how electric current flowed through a vacuum tube. His hypothesis was:

1. If rays are made of charged particles, then an electric field would attract them.

2. If it is a charged particle, then a magnet will affect its motion.

From his work, Thompson proved that the rays were made of negative particles. These particles were later called electrons.

The results of his experimentation produced **Thompson's Model:** The atom is made of negative particles equally mixed in a sphere of positive material.

In 1986, it was discovered that some elements give off particles with a positive charge. These elements have 7,000 times the mass of electrons. The British scientist **Ernest Rutherford** called these **alpha particles**. He used the alpha particles to test Thompson's model. He hammered gold foil until it was less than 1mm thick and then fired alpha particles at the foil. He used a telescope and a screen to locate the alpha particles. His hypothesis was that if Thompson's theory was right, then the alpha particles would pass through the foil in a straight line. He found that most particles passed through as expected. However, some appeared to bounce off in another direction. This could not be explained by Thompson's model. The result of his experiment gave way to **Rutherford's Model:**

1. Most of the atom is empty space. (This explains why most of the alpha particles pass directly through it.)
2. The center of the atom contains a nucleus containing most of the mass and all of the positively charge of the atom.
3. The scattering of particles occurs when they collide with the nucleus.
4. The region of the space outside the nucleus is occupied by electrons.
5. The atom is neutral because the protons in the nucleus equal the electrons in the space outside the nucleus.

Based on Rutherford's model, scientists thought that the electrons of an atom might orbit the nucleus much like the planets orbit the sun. If this is true, they could expect two things:

1. As electrons orbit, they give off light energy continuously. If this light energy is passed through a prism, it would produce a band of color.
2. As the orbiting electrons gave off light, they would lose energy and spiral into the nucleus of the atom causing the atom to collapse. Therefore, the atom would take up no space.

No color band was observed. Instead, lines of color and dark lines were observed. Also, since we know that because matter does in fact take up space, then the orbiting atoms cannot collapse into nothing. Another model was necessary to explain the observations. The Danish scientist **Neils Bohr** created a model in 1913. The results of his model are:

1. Electrons orbit the nucleus, but only certain orbits are allowed. An electron in an allowed orbit will not lose energy.
2. When an electron moves from an outer orbit to an inner orbit, it gives off energy.
3. When an electron moves from an inner orbit to an outer orbit, it absorbs energy.

Bohr's model only explains the very simplest atoms, such as hydrogen. Today's more sophisticated atomic model is based upon how waves react.

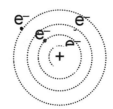

**SKILL 2.7    Identify the major components of the atom and their characteristics and functions.**

An **atom** is a nucleus surrounded by a cloud with moving electrons.

The **nucleus** is the center of the atom. The positive particles inside the nucleus are called **protons.** The mass of a proton is about 2,000 times that of the mass of an electron. The number of protons in the nucleus of an atom is called the **atomic number**. All atoms of the same element have the same atomic number.

**Neutrons** are another type of particle in the nucleus. Neutrons and protons have about the same mass, but neutrons have no charge. Neutrons were discovered because scientists observed that not all atoms in neon gas have the same mass. They had identified isotopes. **Isotopes** of an element have the same number of protons in the nucleus but have different masses. Neutrons explain the difference in mass. They have mass but no charge.

The mass of matter is measured against a standard mass such as the gram. Scientists measure the mass of an atom by comparing it to that of a standard atom. The result is relative mass. The **relative mass** of an atom is its mass expressed in terms of the mass of the standard atom. The isotope of the element carbon is the standard atom. It has six (6) neutrons and is called carbon-12. It is assigned a mass of 12 atomic mass units (amu). Therefore, the **atomic mass unit (amu)** is the standard unit for measuring the mass of an atom. It is equal to the mass of a carbon atom.

The **mass number** of an atom is the sum of its protons and neutrons. In any element, there is a mixture of isotopes, some having slightly more or slightly fewer protons and neutrons. The **atomic mass** of an element is an average of the mass numbers of its atoms.

The following table summarizes the terms used to describe atomic nuclei:

| Term | Example | Meaning | Characteristic |
|------|---------|---------|----------------|
| Atomic Number | # protons (p) | same for all atoms of a given element | Carbon (C) atomic number = 6 (6p) |
| Mass number | # protons + # neutrons (p + n) | changes for different isotopes of an element | C-12 (6p + 6n) C-13 (6p + 7n) |
| Atomic mass | average mass of the atoms of the element | usually not a whole number | atomic mass of carbon equals 12.011 |

Each atom has an equal number of electrons (negative) and protons (positive). Therefore, atoms are neutral. Electrons orbiting the nucleus occupy energy levels that are arranged in order and the electrons tend to occupy the lowest energy level available. A **stable electron arrangement** is an atom that has all of its electrons in the lowest possible energy levels.

Each energy level holds a maximum number of electrons. However, an atom with more than one level does not hold more than 8 electrons in its outermost shell.

| Level | Name | Max. # of Electrons |
|-------|------|---------------------|
| First | K shell | 2 |
| Second | L shell | 8 |
| Third | M shell | 18 |
| Fourth | N shell | 32 |

This can help explain why chemical reactions occur. Atoms react with each other when their outer levels are unfilled. When atoms either exchange or share electrons with each other, these energy levels become filled and the atom becomes more stable.

As an electron gains energy, it moves from one energy level to a higher energy level. The electron cannot leave one level until it has enough energy to reach the next level. **Excited electrons** are electrons that have absorbed energy and have moved farther from the nucleus.

Electrons can also lose energy. When they do, they fall to a lower level. However, they can only fall to the lowest level that has room for them. This explains why atoms do not collapse.

### SKILL 2.8    Identify groups of elements in the periodic table, given chemical or physical properties.

The **periodic table of elements** is an arrangement of the elements in rows and columns so that it is easy to locate elements with similar properties. The elements of the modern periodic table are arranged in numerical order by atomic number.

The **periods** are the rows down the left side of the table. They are called first period, second period, etc. The columns of the periodic table are called **groups**, or **families.** Elements in a family have similar properties.

There are three types of elements that are grouped by color: metals, nonmetals, and metalloids.

**Element Key**

Atomic
Number

↓

Electron    →
Arrangement **

Symbol of   →
Element

Average
Atomic
Mass

↑

Element
Name

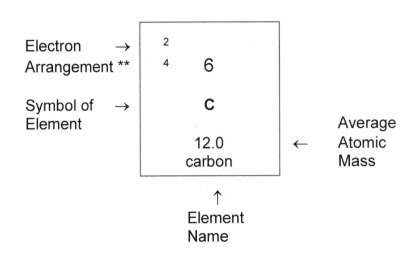

** Number of electrons on each level. Top number represents the innermost level.

## Periodic Table of the Elements

Humdan/Shutterstock.com

### SKILL 2.9 Apply knowledge of the periodic table to determine placement of elements.

The periodic table arranges metals into families with similar properties. The periodic table has its columns marked IA - VIIIA. These are the traditional group numbers. Arabic numbers 1 - 18 are also used, as suggested by the Union of Physicists and Chemists. The Arabic numerals will be used in this text.

### Metals:

With the exception of hydrogen, all elements in Group 1 are **alkali metals**. These metals are shiny, softer, and less dense, and the most chemically active.

Group 2 metals are the **alkaline earth metals.** They are harder, denser, have higher melting points, and are chemically active.

The **transition elements** can be found by finding the periods (rows) from 4 to 7 under the groups (columns) 3 - 12. They are metals that do not show a range of properties as you move across the chart. They are hard and have high melting points. Compounds of these elements are colorful, such as silver, gold, and mercury.

Elements can be combined to make metallic objects. An **alloy** is a mixture of two or more elements having properties of metals. The elements do not have to be all metals. For instance, steel is made up of the metal iron and the non-metal carbon.

### Nonmetals:

Nonmetals are not as easy to recognize as metals because they do not always share physical properties. However, in general the properties of nonmetals are the opposite of metals. They are not shiny, are brittle, and are not good conductors of heat and electricity.

Nonmetals are solids, gases, and one liquid (bromine).

Nonmetals have four to eight electrons in their outermost energy levels and tend to attract electrons to their outer energy levels. As a result, the outer levels usually are filled with eight electrons. This difference in the number of electrons is what caused the differences between metals and nonmetals. The outstanding chemical property of nonmetals is that react with metals.

The **halogens** can be found in Group 17. Halogens combine readily with metals to form salts. Table salt, fluoride toothpaste, and bleach all have an element from the halogen family.

The **Noble Gases** got their name from the fact that they did not react chemically with other elements, much like the nobility did not mix with the masses. These gases (found in Group 18) will only combine with other elements under very specific conditions. They are **inert** (inactive).

In recent years, scientists have found this to be only generally true, since chemists have been able to prepare compounds of krypton and xenon.

### Metalloids:

**Metalloids** have properties in between metals and nonmetals. They can be found in Groups 13 - 16, but do not occupy the entire group. They are arranged in stair steps across the groups.

Physical Properties:

1. All are solids having the appearance of metals.
2. All are white or gray, but not shiny.
3. They will conduct electricity, but not as well as a metal.

Chemical Properties:

1. They have some characteristics of metals and nonmetals.
2. Properties do not follow patterns like metals and nonmetals. Each must be studied individually.

Boron is the first element in Group 13. It is a poor conductor of electricity at low temperatures. However, increase its temperature and it becomes a good conductor. By comparison, metals, which are good conductors, lose their ability as they are heated. It is because of this property that boron is so useful. Boron is a semiconductor. **Semiconductors** are used in electrical devices that have to function at temperatures too high for metals.

**Silicon** is the second element in Group 14. It is also a semiconductor and is found in great abundance in the earth's crust. Sand is made of a silicon compound, silicon dioxide. Silicon is also used in the manufacture of glass and cement.

### SKILL 2.10   Compare covalent and ionic bonding.

The outermost electrons in the atoms are called **valence electrons.** Because they are the ones involved in the bonding process, they determine the properties of the element.

A **chemical bond** is a force of attraction that holds atoms together. When atoms are bonded chemically, they cease to have their individual properties. For instance, hydrogen and oxygen combine into water and no longer look like hydrogen and oxygen. They look like water.

A **covalent bond** is formed when two atoms share electrons. Recall that atoms whose outer shells are not filled with electrons are unstable. When they are unstable, they readily combine with other unstable atoms. By combining and sharing electrons, they act as a single unit. Covalent bonding happens among nonmetals. Covalent bonds are always polar when between two non-identical atoms.

**Covalent compounds** are compounds whose atoms are joined by covalent bonds. Table sugar, methane, and ammonia are examples of covalent compounds.

An **ionic bond** is a bond formed by the transfer of electrons. It happens when metals and nonmetals bond. Before chlorine and sodium combine, the sodium has one valence electron and chlorine has seven. Neither valence shell is filled, but the chlorine's valence shell is almost full. During the reaction, the sodium gives one valence electron to the chlorine atom. Both atoms then have filled shells and are stable. Something else has happened during the bonding. Before the bonding, both atoms were neutral. When one electron was transferred, it upset the balance of protons and electrons in each atom. The chlorine atom took on one extra electron and the sodium atom released one atom. The atoms have now become ions. **Ions** are atoms with an unequal number of protons and electrons. To determine whether the ion is positive or negative, compare the number of protons (+charge) to the electrons (-charge). If there are more electrons the ion will be negative. If there are more protons, the ion will be positive.

Compounds that result from the transfer of metal atoms to nonmetal atoms are called **ionic compounds.** Sodium chloride (table salt), sodium hydroxide (drain cleaner), and potassium chloride (salt substitute) are examples of ionic compounds.

Spontaneous diffusion occurs when random motion leads particles to increase entropy by equalizing concentrations. Particles tend to move into places of lower concentration. For example, sodium will move into a cell if the concentration is greater outside than inside the cell. Spontaneous diffusion keeps cells balanced.

**SKILL 2.11    Identify types of chemical reactions and their characteristics**

There are four kinds of chemical reactions:

In a **composition reaction**, two or more substances combine to form a compound.

A + B  $\rightarrow$  AB
i.e. Silver and sulfur yield silver sulfide.

In a **decomposition reaction**, a compound breaks down into two or more simpler substances.

AB $\rightarrow$ A + B
i.e. Water breaks down into hydrogen and oxygen.

In a **single replacement reaction**, a free element replaces an element that is part of a compound.

A + BX $\rightarrow$ AX + B
i.e. Iron plus copper sulfate yields iron sulfate plus copper.

In a **double replacement reaction**, parts of two compounds replace each other. In this case, the compounds seem to switch partners.

AX + BY $\rightarrow$ AY + BX
i.e. Sodium chloride plus mercury nitrate yields sodium nitrate plus mercury chloride.

**COMPETENCY 3.0     KNOWLEDGE OF EARTH/SPACE SCIENCE**

**SKILL 3.1     Explain plate tectonics theory and continental drift as each relates to geologic history or phenomena (e.g., volcanism and diastrophism).**

Data obtained from many sources led scientists to develop the theory of plate tectonics. This theory is the most current model that explains not only the movement of the continents, but also the changes in the earth's crust caused by internal forces.

Plates are rigid blocks of earth's crust and upper mantle. These rigid solid blocks make up the lithosphere. The earth's lithosphere is broken into nine large sections and several small ones. These moving slabs are called plates. The major plates are named after the continents they are "transporting."

The plates float on and move with a layer of hot, plastic-like rock in the upper mantle. Geologists believe that the heat currents circulating within the mantle cause this plastic zone of rock to slowly flow, carrying along the overlying crustal plates.

Movement of these crustal plates creates areas where the plates diverge as well as areas where the plates converge. In the Mid-Atlantic is a major area of divergence. Currents of hot mantle rock rise and separate at this point of divergence creating new oceanic crust at the rate of 2 to 10 centimeters per year. Convergence is when the oceanic crust collides with either another oceanic plate or a continental plate. The oceanic crust sinks forming an enormous trench and generating volcanic activity. Convergence also includes continent-to-continent plate collisions. When two plates slide past one another, a transform fault is created.

These movements produce many major features of the earth's surface, such as mountain ranges, volcanoes, and earthquake zones. Most of these features are located at plate boundaries, where the plates interact by spreading apart, pressing together, or sliding past each other. These movements are very slow, averaging only a few centimeters a year.

Boundaries form between spreading plates where the crust is forced apart in a process called rifting. Rifting generally occurs at mid-ocean ridges. Rifting can also take place within a continent, splitting the continent into smaller landmasses that drift away from each other, thereby forming an ocean basin (Red Sea) between them. As the seafloor spreading takes place, new material is added to the inner edges of the separating plates. In this way, the plates grow larger, and the ocean basin widens. This is the process that broke up the super continent Pangaea and created the Atlantic Ocean.

# CONTINENTAL DRIFT

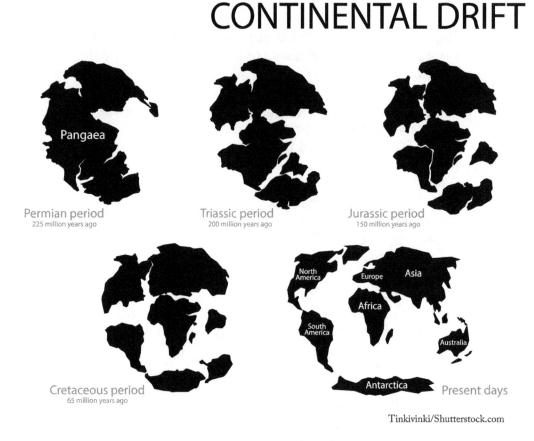

Permian period
225 million years ago

Triassic period
200 million years ago

Jurassic period
150 million years ago

Cretaceous period
65 million years ago

Present days

North America    Europe    Asia    Africa    South America    Australia    Antarctica

Tinkivinki/Shutterstock.com

Boundaries between plates that are colliding are zones of intense crustal activity. When a plate of ocean crust collides with a plate of continental crust, the dense oceanic plate slides under the lighter continental plate and plunges into the mantle. This process is called **subduction**, and the site where it takes place is called a subduction zone. A subduction zone is usually seen on the seafloor as a deep depression called a trench.

The crustal movement, characterized by plates sliding sideways past each other, produces a plate boundary characterized by major faults that are capable of unleashing powerful earthquakes. The San Andreas Fault forms such a boundary between the Pacific Plate and the North American Plate.

**SKILL 3.2**   **Identify characteristics of geologic structures and the mechanisms by which they were formed (e.g. mountains and glaciers).**

**Orogeny** is the term given to natural mountain building.

A mountain is terrain that has been raised high above the surrounding landscape by volcanic action, or some form of tectonic plate collisions. The plate collisions could be intercontinental or ocean floor collisions with a continental crust (subduction). The physical composition of mountains would include igneous, metamorphic, or sedimentary rocks; some may have rock layers that are tilted or distorted by plate collision forces.

There are many different types of mountains. The physical attributes of a mountain range depends upon the angle at which plate movement thrust layers of rock to the surface. Many mountains (Adirondacks, Southern Rockies) were formed along high angle faults.

Folded mountains (Alps, Himalayas) are produced by the folding of rock layers during their formation. The Himalayas are the highest mountains in the world and contains Mount Everest, which rises almost 9 km above sea level. The Himalayas were formed when India collided with Asia. The movement which created this collision is still in process at the rate of a few centimeters per year.

Fault-block mountains (Utah, Arizona, and New Mexico) are created when plate movement produces tension forces instead of compression forces. The area under tension produces normal faults, and rock along these faults is displaced upward.

Dome mountains are formed as magma tries to push up through the crust but fails to break the surface. Dome mountains resemble a huge blister on the earth's surface.

Upwarped mountains (Black Hills of South Dakota) are created in association with a broad arching of the crust. They can also be formed by rock thrust upward along high angle faults.

Volcanic mountains are built up by successive deposits of volcanic materials.

Volcanism is the term given to the movement of magma through the crust and its emergence as lava onto the earth's surface.

An active volcano is one that is presently erupting or building to an eruption. A dormant volcano is one that is between eruptions but still shows signs of internal activity that might lead to an eruption in the future. An extinct volcano is said to be no longer capable of erupting. Most of the world's active volcanoes are found along the rim of the Pacific Ocean, which is also a major earthquake zone. This curving belt of active faults and volcanoes is often called the Ring of Fire.

The world's best known volcanic mountains include Mount Etna in Italy and Mount Kilimanjaro in Africa. The Hawaiian Islands are the tops of a chain of volcanic mountains that rise from the ocean floor.

There are three types of volcanic mountains: shield volcanoes, cinder cones and composite volcanoes.

**Shield Volcanoes** are associated with quiet eruptions. Lava emerges from the vent or opening in the crater and flows freely out over the earth's surface until it cools and hardens into a layer of igneous rock. A repeated lava flow builds this type of volcano into the largest volcanic mountain. Mauna Loa, found in Hawaii, is the largest volcano on earth.

**Cinder Cone Volcanoes** associated with explosive eruptions as lava is hurled high into the air in a spray of droplets of various sizes. These droplets cool and harden into cinders and particles of ash before falling to the ground. The ash and cinder pile up around the vent to form a steep, cone-shaped hill called the cinder cone. Cinder cone volcanoes are relatively small but may form quite rapidly.

**Composite Volcanoes** are built by both lava flows and layers of ash and cinders. Mount Fuji in Japan, Mount St. Helens in Washington, USA, and Mount Vesuvius in Italy are all famous composite volcanoes.

## Mechanisms of Producing Mountains

Mountains are produced by different types of mountain-building processes. Most major mountain ranges are formed by the processes of folding and faulting.

**Folded Mountains** are produced by folding of rock layers. Crustal movements may press horizontal layers of sedimentary rock together from the sides, squeezing them into wavelike folds. Up-folded sections of rock are called anticlines; down-folded sections of rock are called synclines. The Appalachian Mountains are an example of folded mountains with long ridges and valleys in a series of anticlines and synclines formed by folded rock layers.

Faults are fractures in Earth's crust, which have been created by either tension or compression forces transmitted through the crust. These forces are produced by the movement of separate blocks of crust.

Faultings are categorized based on the relative movement between the blocks on both sides of the fault plane. The movement can be horizontal, vertical or oblique.

**A dip-slip fault** occurs when the movement of the plates is vertical and opposite. The displacement is in the direction of the inclination, or dip, of the fault. Dip-slip faults are classified as normal faults when the rock above the fault plane moves down, relative to the rock below.

**Reverse faults** are created when the rock above the fault plane moves up relative to the rock below. Reverse faults having a very low angle to the horizontal are also referred to as thrust faults.

Faults in which the dominant displacement is horizontal movement along the trend or strike (length) of the fault are called strike-slip faults. When a large strike-slip fault is associated with plate boundaries, it is called a transform fault. The San Andreas Fault in California is a well-known transform fault.

Faults that have both vertical and horizontal movement are called oblique-slip faults.

When lava cools, igneous rock is formed. This formation can occur either above ground or below ground.

**Intrusive rock** includes any igneous rock that was formed below the earth's surface.  Batholiths are the largest structures of intrusive type rock and are composed of near-granite materials; they are the core of the Sierra Nevada Mountains.

**Extrusive rock** includes any igneous rock that was formed at the earth's surface.

**Dikes** are old lava tubes formed when magma entered a vertical fracture and hardened. Sometimes, magma squeezes between two rock layers and hardens into a thin horizontal sheet called a sill. A **laccolith** is formed in much the same way as a sill, but the magma that creates a **laccolith** is very thick and does not flow easily. It pools and forces the overlying strata, creating an obvious surface dome.

A **caldera** is normally formed by the collapse of the top of a volcano. This collapse can be caused by a massive explosion that destroys the cone and empties most if not all the magma chamber below the volcano. The cone collapses into the empty magma chamber, forming a caldera.

An inactive volcano may have magma solidified in its pipe. This structure, called a volcanic neck, is resistant to erosion and today may be the only visible evidence of the past presence of an active volcano.

When lava cools, igneous rock is formed. This formation can occur either above ground or below ground.

### Glaciation

A continental glacier covered a large part of North America during the most recent ice age. Evidence of this glacial coverage remains as abrasive grooves, large boulders from northern environments dropped in southerly locations, glacial troughs created by the rounding out of steep valleys by glacial scouring, and the remains of glacial sources called **cirques** that were created by frost wedging the rock at the bottom of the glacier. Remains of plants and animals found in warm climate have been discovered in the moraines and out wash plains help to support the theory of periods of warmth during the past ice ages.

The Ice Age began about 2 -3 million years ago. This age saw the advancement and retreat of glacial ice over millions of years. Theories relating to the origin of glacial activity include Plate Tectonics, where it can be demonstrated that some continental masses, now in temperate climates, were at one time blanketed by ice and snow. Another theory involves changes in the earth's orbit around the sun, changes in the angle of the earth's axis, and the wobbling of the earth's axis. Support for the validity of this theory has come from deep ocean research that indicates a correlation between climatic sensitive microorganisms and the changes in the earth's orbital status.

About 12,000 years ago, a vast sheet of ice covered a large part of the northern United States. This huge, frozen mass had moved southward from the northern regions of Canada as several large bodies of slow-moving ice, or glaciers. A time period in which glaciers advance over a large portion of a continent is called an ice age. A glacier is a large mass of ice that moves or flows over the land in response to gravity. Glaciers form among high mountains and in other cold regions.

There are two main types of glaciers: valley glaciers and continental glaciers. Erosion by valley glaciers is characteristic of U-shaped erosion. They produce sharp peaked mountains such as the Matterhorn in Switzerland. Erosion by continental glaciers often rides over mountains in their paths, leaving smoothed, rounded mountains and ridges.

### SKILL 3.3    Explain the formation of fossils and how they are used to interpret the past.

Fossils are the remains or traces of an ancient organism that have been preserved naturally in the Earth's crust. Sedimentary rocks usually are rich sources of fossil remains. Those fossils found in layers of sediment were embedded in the slowly forming sedimentary rock strata. The oldest fossils known are the traces of 3.5-billion year old bacteria found in sedimentary rocks. Few fossils are found in metamorphic rock and virtually none found in igneous rocks. The magma is so hot that any organism trapped in the magma is destroyed.

The fossil remains of a woolly mammoth embedded in ice were found by a group of Russian explorers. However, the best-preserved animal remains have been discovered in natural tar pits. When an animal accidentally fell into the tar, it became trapped sinking to the bottom. Preserved bones of the saber-toothed cat have been found in tar pits.

Prehistoric insects have been found trapped in ancient amber or fossil resin that was excreted by some extinct species of pine trees.

Fossil molds are the hollow spaces in a rock previously occupied by bones or shells. A fossil cast is a fossil mold that fills with sediments or minerals that later hardens forming a cast.

Fossil tracks are imprints in hardened mud, left behind by the birds or animals.

### SKILL 3.4 Identify the order of geologic time periods, life forms present in each period and methods for determining geologic age.

The biological history of the earth is partitioned into four major Eras that are further divided into major periods. The latter periods are refined into groupings called Epochs.

Earth's history extends over more than four billion years and is reckoned in terms of a scale. Paleontologists who study the history of the Earth have divided this huge period of time into four large time units called eons. Eons are divided into smaller units of time called eras. An era refers to a time interval in which particular plants and animals were dominant, or present in great abundance. The end of an era is most often characterized by (1) a general uplifting of the crust, (2) the extinction of the dominant plants or animals, and (3) the appearance of new life forms.

Each era is divided into several smaller divisions of time called periods. Some periods are divided into smaller time units called epochs.

### Methods of Geologic Dating

Estimates of the Earth's age have been made possible with the discovery of **radioactivity** and the invention of instruments that can measure the amount of radioactivity in rocks. The use of radioactivity to make accurate determinations of Earth's age is called absolute dating. This process depends upon comparing the amount of radioactive material in a rock with the amount that has decayed into another element. Studying the radiation given off by atoms of radioactive elements is the most accurate method of measuring the Earth's age. These atoms are unstable and are continuously breaking down or undergoing decay. The radioactive element that decays is called the parent element. The new element that results from the radioactive decay of the parent element is called the daughter element.

The time required for one half of a given amount of a radioactive element to decay is called the half-life of that element or compound.

Geologists commonly use carbon dating to calculate the age of a fossil substance.

## Infer the History of an Area Using Geologic Evidence

The determination of the age of rocks by cataloging their composition has been outmoded since the middle 1800s. Today, a sequential history can be determined by the fossil content (principle of fossil succession) of a rock system as well as its superposition within a range of systems. This classification process was termed stratigraphy and permitted the construction of a geologic column in which rock systems are arranged in their correct chronological order.

## Principles of Catastrophism and Uniformitarianism

**Uniformitarianism** - A fundamental concept in modern geology. It simply states that the physical, chemical, and biological laws that operated in the geologic past operate in the same way today. The forces and processes that we observe presently shaping our planet have been at work for a very long time. This idea is commonly stated as "the present is the key to the past."

**Catastrophism** - The concept that the earth was shaped by catastrophic events of a short-term nature.

**SKILL 3.5    Interpret various geologic maps, including topographic and weather maps that contain symbols, scales, legends, directions, time zones, latitudes, and longitudes.**

## Decode Map Symbols

**Hachures** are depressions or tiny comb-like markings that point inward from the contour line toward the bottom of the depression. A contour line that has hachures is called a depression contour.

A system of imaginary lines has been developed that helps people describe exact locations on Earth. Looking at a globe of Earth, you will see lines drawn on it. The equator is drawn around Earth halfway between the North and South Poles. Latitude is a term used to describe distance in degrees north or south of the equator.  Lines of latitude are drawn east and west parallel to the equator. Degrees of latitude range from 0 at the equator to 90 at either the North Pole or South Pole. Lines of latitude are also called parallels.

Lines drawn north and south at right angles to the equator and from pole to pole are called meridians. Longitude is a term used to describe distances in degrees east or west of a 0° meridian. The prime meridian is the 0° meridian and it passes through Greenwich, England.

Time zones are determined by longitudinal lines. Each time zone represents one hour. Since there are 24 hours in one complete rotation of the Earth, there are 24 international time zones. Each time zone is roughly 15° wide. While time zones are based on meridians, they do not strictly follow lines of longitude. Time zone boundaries are subject to political decisions and have been moved around cities and other areas at the whim of the electorate.

The International Date Line is the 180° meridian and it is on the opposite side of the world from the prime meridian. The International Date Line is one-half of one day or 12 time zones from the prime meridian. If you were traveling west across the International Date Line, you would lose one day. If you were traveling east across the International Date Line, you would gain one day.

## Principles of Contouring

A contour line is a line on a map representing an imaginary line on the ground that has the same elevation above sea level along its entire length. Contour intervals usually are given in even numbers or as a multiple of five. In mapping mountains, a large contour interval is used. Small contour intervals may be used where there are small differences in elevation.

Relief describes how much variation in elevation an area has. Rugged or high relief describes an area of many hills and valleys. Gentle or low relief describes a plain area or a coastal region. Five general rules should be remembered in studying contour lines on a map.

1. Contour lines close around hills and basins or depressions. Hachure lines are used to show depressions. Hachures are short lines placed at right angles to the contour line and they always point toward the lower elevation.

2. Contours lines never cross. Contour lines are sometimes very close together. Each contour line represents a certain height above sea level.

3. Contour lines appear on both sides of an area where the slope reverses direction. Contour lines show where an imaginary horizontal plane would slice through a hillside or cut both sides of a valley.

4. Contours lines form V's that point upstream when they cross streams. Streams cut beneath the general elevation of the land surface, and contour lines follow a valley.

5.  All contours lines either close (connect) or extend to the edge of the map. No map is large enough to have all its contour lines close.

## Interpret Maps and Imagery

Like photographs, maps readily display information that would be impractical to express in words. Maps that show the shape of the land are called topographic maps. Topographic maps, which are also referred to as quadrangles, are generally classified according to publication scale. Relief refers to the difference in elevation between any two points. Maximum relief refers to the difference in elevation between the highest and lowest points in the area being considered. Relief determines the contour interval, which is the difference in elevation between succeeding contour lines that are used on topographic maps.

Map scales express the relationship between distance or area on the map to the true distance or area on the earth's surface. It is expressed as so many feet (miles, meters, km, or degrees) per inch (cm) of map.

## SKILL 3.6 Identify types of currents and tides and how each is produced.

World weather patterns are greatly influenced by ocean surface currents in the upper layer of the ocean. These currents continuously move along the ocean surface in specific directions. Ocean currents that flow deep below the surface are called sub-surface currents. These currents are influenced by such factors as the location of landmasses in the current's path and the earth's rotation.

Surface currents are caused by winds and classified by temperature. Cold currents originate in the Polar regions and flow through surrounding water that is measurably warmer. Those currents with a higher temperature than the surrounding water are called warm currents and can be found near the equator. These currents follow swirling routes around the ocean basins and the equator. The Gulf Stream and the California Current are the two main surface currents that flow along the coastlines of the United States. The Gulf Stream is a warm current in the Atlantic Ocean that carries warm water from the equator to the northern parts of the Atlantic Ocean. Benjamin Franklin studied it and named it the Gulf Stream. The California Current is a cold current that originates in the Arctic regions and flows southward along the west coast of the United States.

Differences in water density also create ocean currents. Water found near the bottom of oceans is the coldest and the densest. Water tends to flow from a denser area to a less dense area. These currents that flow because of a difference in the density of the ocean water are called density currents. Water with a higher salinity is denser than water with a lower salinity. Water that has salinity different from the surrounding water may form a density current.

## Knowledge of the Causes and Effects of Waves

The movement of ocean water is caused by the wind, the sun's heat energy, the earth's rotation, the moon's gravitational pull on earth and by underwater earthquakes. Most ocean waves are caused by the impact of winds. Wind blowing over the surface of the ocean transfers energy (friction) to the water and causes waves to form. Waves are also formed by a seismic activity on the ocean floor. A wave formed by an earthquake is called a seismic sea wave. These powerful waves can be very destructive, with wave heights increasing to 30 m or more near the shore. The crest of a wave is its highest point. The trough of a wave is its lowest point. The distance from wave top to wave top is the wavelength. The wave period is the time between the passages of two successive waves.

### SKILL 3.7    Identify characteristics of the seafloor, shorelines, estuaries, and sea zones

## Seafloor

The ocean floor has many of the same features that are found on land. The ocean floor has higher mountains than present on land, extensive plains and deeper canyons than present on land. Oceanographers have named different parts of the ocean floor according to their structure.
The major parts of the ocean floor are:

The **continental shelf** is the sloping part of the continent that is covered with water extending from the shoreline to the continental slope.

The **continental slope** is the steeply sloping area that connects the continental shelf and the deep-ocean floor.

The **continental rise** is the gently sloping surface at the base of the continental slope.

The **abyssal plains** are the flat, level parts of the ocean floor.

A **seamount** is an undersea volcano peak that is at least 1000 m above the ocean floor.

**A guyot** is a submerged flat-topped seamount.

**Mid-ocean ridges** are continuous undersea mountain chains that are found mostly in the middle portions of the oceans.

**Ocean trenches** are long, elongated narrow troughs or depressions formed where ocean floors collide with another section of ocean floor or continent. The deepest trench in the Pacific Ocean is the Marianas Trench, which is about 11 km deep.

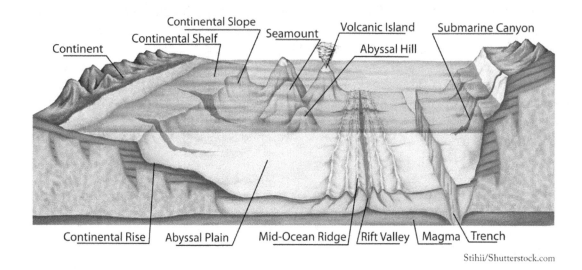

Stihii/Shutterstock.com

*Shorelines*

The shoreline is the boundary where land and sea meet. Shorelines mark the average position of sea level, which is the average height of the sea without consideration of tides and waves. Shorelines are classified according to the way they were formed. The three types of shorelines are: submerged, emergent, and neutral. When the sea has risen, or the land has sunk, a **submerged shoreline** is created. An **emergent shoreline** occurs when sea falls or the land rises. A **neutral shoreline** does not show the features of a submerged or an emergent shoreline. A neutral shoreline is usually observed as a flat and broad beach. A **stack** is an island of resistant rock left after weaker rock is worn away by waves and currents. Waves approaching the beach at a slight angle create a current of water that flows parallel to the shore. This longshore current carries loose sediment almost like a river of sand. A spit is formed when a weak longshore current drops its load of sand as it turns into a bay.

Rip currents are narrow currents that flow seaward at a right angle to the shoreline. These currents are very dangerous to swimmers. Most of the beach sands are composed of grains of resistant material like quartz and orthoclase but coral or basalt are found in some locations. Many beaches have rock fragments that are too large to be classified as sand.

**SKILL 3.8    Identify the Chemical and Physical Properties of Ocean Water**

Seventy percent of Earth's surface is covered with saltwater, which is termed the hydrosphere. The mass of this saltwater is about $1.4 \times 10^{24}$ grams. The ocean waters continuously circulate among different parts of the hydrosphere. There are seven major oceans: the North Atlantic Ocean, South Atlantic Ocean, North Pacific Ocean, South Pacific Ocean, Indian Ocean, Arctic Ocean, and the Antarctic Ocean.

Pure water is a combination of the elements hydrogen and oxygen. These two elements make up about 96.5% of the ocean water. The remaining portion is made up of dissolved solids. The concentration of these dissolved solids determines the water's salinity.

Salinity is the number of grams of these dissolved salts in 1,000 grams of seawater. The average salinity of ocean water is about 3.5%. In other words, one kilogram of seawater contains about 35 grams of salt. Sodium Chloride or salt (NaCl) is the most abundant of the dissolved salts. The dissolved salts also include smaller quantities of magnesium chloride, magnesium and calcium sulfates, and traces of several other salt elements. Salinity varies throughout the world oceans; the total salinity of the oceans varies from place to place and also varies with depth. Salinity is low near river mouths where the ocean mixes with fresh water, and salinity is high in areas of high evaporation rates.

The temperature of the ocean water varies with different latitudes and with ocean depths. Ocean water temperature is about constant to depths of 90 meters (m). The temperature of surface water will drop rapidly from 28° C at the equator to -2° C at the Poles. The freezing point of seawater is lower than the freezing point of pure water. Pure water freezes at 0° C. The dissolved salts in the seawater keep sea water at a freezing point of -2° C. The freezing point of seawater may vary depending on its salinity in a particular location.

The ocean can be divided into three temperature zones. The surface layer consists of relatively warm water and exhibits most of the wave action present. The area where the wind and waves churn and mix the water is called the mixed layer. This is the layer where most living creatures are found due to abundant sunlight and warmth. The second layer is called the thermocline and it becomes increasingly colder as its depth increases. This change is due to the lack of energy from sunlight. The layer below the thermocline continues to the deep dark, very cold, and semi-barren ocean floor.

**Oozes** - The name given to the sediment that contains at least 30% plant or animal shell fragments. Ooze contains calcium carbonate. Deposits that form directly from seawater in the place where they are found are called:

**Authigenic deposits** - Manganese nodules are authigenic deposits found over large areas of the ocean floor.

## Causes for the Formation of Ocean Floor Features

The surface of the earth is in constant motion. This motion is the subject of plate tectonics studies. Major plate separation lines lie along the ocean floors. As these plates separate, molten rock rises, continuously forming new ocean crust and creating new and taller mountain ridges under the ocean. The Mid-Atlantic Range, which divides the Atlantic Ocean basin into two nearly equal parts, shows mapping-based evidence of these deep-ocean floor changes.

Seamounts are formed by underwater volcanoes. Seamounts and volcanic islands are found in long chains on the ocean floor. They are formed when the movement of an oceanic plate positions a plate section over a stationary hot spot located deep in the mantle. Magma rising from the hot spot punches through the plate and forms a volcano. The Hawaiian Islands are examples of volcanic island chains.

Magma that rises to produce a curving chain of volcanic islands is called an island arc. An example of an island arc is the Lesser Antilles chain in the Caribbean Sea.

## SKILL 3.9    Identify the major groups of rocks and processes by which each is formed.

Three major subdivisions of rocks are sedimentary, metamorphic and igneous.

### Lithification of Sedimentary Rocks:

When fluid sediments are transformed into solid sedimentary rocks, the process is known as lithification. One very common process affecting sediments is compaction where the weights of overlying materials compress and compact the deeper sediments. The compaction process leads to cementation.
**Cementation** is when sediments are converted to sedimentary rock.

### Factors in Crystallization of Igneous Rocks:

**Igneous rocks** can be classified according to their texture, their composition, and the way they formed.

Molten rock is called **magma**. When molten rock pours out onto the surface of Earth, it is called lava.

As magma cools, the elements and compounds begin to form crystals. The slower the magma cools, the larger the crystals grow. Rocks with large crystals are said to have a coarse-grained texture. Granite is an example of a coarse-grained rock. Rocks that cool rapidly before any crystals can form have a glassy texture such as obsidian, also commonly known as volcanic glass.

**Metamorphic rocks** are formed by high temperatures and great pressures. The process by which the rocks undergo these changes is called metamorphism. The outcome of metamorphic changes include deformation by extreme heat and pressure, compaction, destruction of the original characteristics of the parent rock, bending and folding while in a plastic stage, and the emergence of completely new and different minerals due to chemical reactions with heated water and dissolved minerals.

Metamorphic rocks are classified into two groups, foliated (leaflike) rocks and unfoliated rocks. Foliated rocks consist of compressed, parallel bands of minerals, which give the rocks a striped appearance. Examples of such rocks include; slate, schist, and gneiss. Unfoliated rocks are not banded, and examples of such include quartzite, marble, and anthracite rocks.

**Minerals** are natural, non-living solids with a definite chemical composition and a crystalline structure. **Ores** are minerals or rock deposits that can be mined for a profit. **Rocks** are earth materials made of one or more minerals. **Rock facies** is a rock group that differs from comparable rocks (as in composition, age or fossil content).

**Characteristics by which Minerals are Classified:**

Minerals must adhere to five criteria. They must be (1) non-living, (2) formed in nature, (3) solid in form, (4) made up of atoms that form a crystalline pattern, and (5) somewhat fixed in their chemical composition...

There are over 3000 minerals in Earth's crust. Minerals are classified by composition. The major groups of minerals are silicates, carbonates, oxides, sulfides, sulfates, and halides. The largest group of minerals is the silicates. Silicates are made of silicon, oxygen, and one or more other elements.

## SKILL 3.10   Knowledge of Soil Types and Properties

Soils are composed of particles of sand, clay, various minerals, tiny living organisms, and humus, plus the decayed remains of plants and animals. Soils are divided into three classes according to their texture. These classes are sandy soils, clay soils, and loamy soils.

Sandy soils are gritty, and their particles do not bind together firmly. Sandy soils are porous; water passes through them rapidly. Sandy soils do not hold much water.

Clay soils are smooth and greasy; their particles bind together firmly. Clay soils are moist and usually do not allow water to pass through easily.

Loamy soils feel somewhat like velvet and their particles clump together. Loamy soils are made up of sand, clay, and silt. Loamy soils hold water, but some water can pass through.

Soils are grouped into three major types based upon their composition: pedalfers, pedocals and laterites.

Pedalfers form in the humid, temperate climate of the eastern United States. Pedalfer soils contain large amounts of iron oxide and aluminum-rich clays, making the soil a brown to reddish brown color. This soil supports forest-type vegetation.

Pedocals are found in the western United States, where the climate is dry and temperate. These soils are rich in calcium carbonate. This type of soil supports grasslands and brush vegetation.

Laterites are found where the climate is wet and tropical. Large amounts of water flows through this soil. Laterites are red-orange soils rich in iron and aluminum oxides. There is little humus and this soil is not very fertile.

## SKILL 3.11    Identify renewable and nonrenewable natural resources.

A **renewable resource** is one that is replaced naturally. Living renewable resources would be plants and animals. Plants are renewable because they grow and reproduce. Sometimes, renewal of the resource doesn't keep up with the demand. Such is the case with trees. Since the housing industry uses lumber for frames and homebuilding, they are often cut down faster than new trees can grow. Now there are specific tree farms. Special methods allow trees to grow faster.

A second renewable resource is animals. They renew by the process of reproduction. Some wild animals need protection on refuges. As the population of humans increases, resources are used faster. Cattle are used for their hides and for food. Some animals like deer are killed for sport. Each state has an environmental protection agency with divisions of forest management and wildlife management.

Non-living renewable resources would be water, air, and soil. Water is renewed in a natural cycle called the water cycle. Air is a mixture of gases. Oxygen is given off by plants and taken in by animals that in turn expel the carbon dioxide that the plants need. Soil is another renewable resource. Fertile soil is rich in minerals. When plants grow, they remove the minerals and make the soil less fertile. Chemical treatments are one way or renewing the composition. It is also accomplished naturally when the plants decay back into the soil. The plant material is used to make compost to mix with the soil.

**Nonrenewable** resources are not easily replaced in a timely fashion. Minerals are nonrenewable resources. Quartz, mica, salt and sulfur are some examples. Mining depletes these resources, so society may benefit by glass from quartz, electronic equipment from mica, and salt has many uses. Sulfur is used in medicine, fertilizers, paper, and matches.

Metals are among the most widely used nonrenewable resource. Metals must be separated from the ore. Iron is our most important ore. Gold, silver and copper are often found in a purer form called native metals.

### SKILL 3.12 Apply knowledge of the processes of erosion, weathering, transportation and deposition.

**Erosion** is the inclusion and transportation of surface materials by another moveable material, usually water, wind, or ice. The most important cause of erosion is running water. Streams, rivers, tides and such are constantly at work, removing weathered fragments of bedrock and carrying them away from their original location.

A stream erodes bedrock by the grinding action of the sand, pebbles and other rock fragments. This grinding against each other is called abrasion.

Streams also erode rocks by dissolving or absorbing their minerals. Limestone and marble are readily dissolved by streams.

The breaking down of rocks at or near Earth's surface is known as **weathering**. Weathering breaks down these rocks into smaller and smaller pieces. There are two types of weathering: physical weathering and chemical weathering.

Physical weathering is the process by which rocks are broken down into smaller fragments without undergoing any change in chemical composition. Physical weathering is mainly caused by the freezing of water, the expansion of rock, and the activities of plants and animals.

Frost wedging is the cycle of daytime thawing and refreezing at night. This cycle causes large rock masses, especially the rocks exposed on mountain tops, to be broken into smaller pieces.

The peeling away of the outer layers from a rock is called exfoliation. Rounded mountain tops are called exfoliation domes and have been formed in this way.

Chemical weathering is the breaking down of rocks through changes in their chemical composition. An example would be the change of feldspar in granite to clay. Water, oxygen, and carbon dioxide are the main agents of chemical weathering. When water and carbon dioxide combine chemically, they produce a weak acid that breaks down rocks.

### SKILL 3.13   Identify characteristics of the sun and other stars and devices and techniques for collecting data about stars.

The **sun** is considered the nearest star to earth that produces solar energy by the process of nuclear fusion; hydrogen gas is converted to helium gas. Energy flows out of the core to the surface, radiation then escapes into space.

Parts of the sun include: (1) **core**, the inner portion of the sun where fusion takes place; (2) **photosphere**, considered the surface of the sun which produces **sunspots** (cool, dark areas that can be seen on its surface); (3) **chromosphere**, where hydrogen gas causes this portion to be red in color; **solar flares** (sudden brightness of the chromosphere) and **solar prominences** (gases that shoot outward from the chromosphere) found in the chromosphere; and (4) **corona**, the transparent area of sun visible only during a total eclipse.

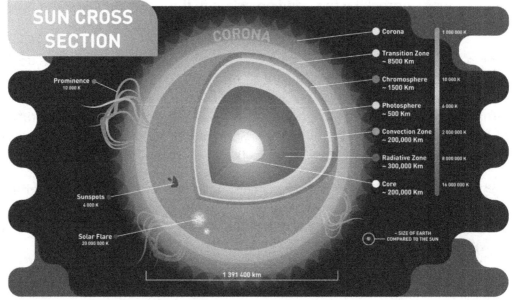

VectorMine/Shutterstock.com

**Solar radiation** is energy traveling from the sun that radiates into space. **Solar flares** produce excited protons and electrons that shoot outward from the chromosphere at great speeds reaching earth. These particles disturb radio reception and also affect the magnetic field on earth.

**Knowledge of Telescope Types**

Galileo was the first person to use telescopes to observer the solar system. He invented the first refracting telescope. A **refracting telescope** uses lenses to bend light rays in focusing the image.

Sir Isaac Newton invented the **reflecting telescope** using mirrors to gather light rays on a curved mirror, which produces a small focused image.

The world's largest telescope is in Mauna Kea, Hawaii. It uses multiple-mirrors to gather light rays.

The **Hubble space telescope** uses a **single-reflector mirror**. It provides an opportunity for astronomers to observe objects seven times farther away even those objects that are 50 times fainter better than any other telescope on earth. There are future plans to make repairs and install new mirrors and other equipment on the Hubble space telescope.

Refracting and reflecting telescopes are considered **optical telescopes** since they gather visible light and focus it to produce images. A different type of telescope that collects invisible radio waves created by the sun and stars is called a **radio telescope.**

**Radio telescopes** consists of a reflector or dish with special receivers. The reflector collects radio waves that are created by the sun and stars. There are many advantages to using a radio telescope. It can receive signals 24 hours a day, operate in any kind of weather, and not deteriorate in performance due to interference from dust particles or clouds. The most impressive aspect of the radio telescope is its ability to detect objects from great distances in space.

The world's largest radio telescope is in Arecibo, Puerto Rico. It has a collecting dish antenna of more than 300 meters in diameter.

**Use of Spectral Analysis to Identify or Infer Features of Stars or Star Systems.**

The **spectroscope** is a device or an attachment for telescopes that is used to separate white light into a series of different colors by wavelengths. This series of colors of light is called a **spectrum**. A **spectrograph** can photograph a spectrum. Wavelengths of light have distinctive colors. The color red has the longest wavelength and violet has the shortest wavelength. Wavelengths are arranged to form an **electromagnetic spectrum**, (see figure 3.18a); they range from very long radio waves to very short gamma rays. Visible light covers a small portion of the electromagnetic spectrum. Spectroscopes observe the spectra, temperatures, pressures, and also the movement of stars. The movements of stars indicate if they are moving toward or away from earth.

If a star is moving towards earth, light waves compress and the wavelengths of light seem shorter. This will cause the entire spectrum to move towards the blue or violet end of the spectrum. This spectral shift to the blue or violet spectrum observed on the electromagnetic spectrum.

If a star is moving away from Earth, light waves expand and the wavelengths of light seem longer. This will cause the entire spectrum to move toward the red end of the spectrum. This spectral shift to the red spectrum is observed on the electromagnetic spectrum. Also, when something is moving further from you, and the wavelength observed now appears longer, it will shift to the red side of the spectrum.

### Knowledge of Astronomical Measurement

The three formulas astronomers use for calculating distances in space are: (1) the **AU or astronomical unit**, (2) **the LY or light year,** and (3) **the parsec**. It is important to remember that these units are measurements of distances, not measurements of time.

The distance between Earth and the sun is about $150 \times 10^6$ km. This distance is known as an astronomical unit or AU. This formula is used to measure distances within the solar system; it is not used to measure time.

The distance light travels in one year is called a light year and is $9.5 \times 10^{12}$ km. This formula is used to measure distances in space; it does not measure time. Large distances are measured in parsecs. One parsec equals 3.26 light-years, not time.

There are approximately 63,000 AU's in one light year or,

$9.5 \times 10^{12}$ km/ $150 \times 10^6$ km $= 6.3 \times 10^4$ AU

### SKILL 3.14 Identify the components of the solar system and their characteristics and relationships to each other.

There are nine planets in our solar system: Mercury, Venus, Earth, Mars, Jupiter, Saturn, Uranus, Neptune, and Pluto. Pluto was an established planet in our solar system, but as of summer 2006, its status is now considered a 'dwarf planet'. The planets are divided into two groups based on distance from the sun. The inner planets include: Mercury, Venus, Earth, and Mars. The outer planets include: Jupiter, Saturn, Uranus and Neptune.

## Planets

**Mercury** -- The closest planet to the sun. Its surface has craters and rocks. The atmosphere is composed of hydrogen, helium and sodium. Mercury was named after the Roman messenger God.

**Venus** -- Has a slow rotation when compared to Earth. It has the slowest rotation when compared to the rest of the planets. Venus and Uranus rotate in opposite directions from the other planets. This opposite rotation is called retrograde rotation. The surface of Venus is not visible due to the extensive cloud cover. The atmosphere is composed primarily of carbon dioxide. Sulfuric acid droplets in the dense cloud cover give Venus a yellow appearance. Venus has a greater greenhouse effect than observed on Earth. The dense clouds, combined with carbon dioxide, trap heat. Venus was named after the Roman Goddess of love.

**Earth** -- Considered a water planet, with 70% of its surface covered with water. Gravity holds the masses of water in place. The different temperatures observed on Earth allow for the different states of water—solid, liquid, and gas—to exist. The atmosphere is composed mainly of oxygen and nitrogen. Earth is the only planet that is known to support life.

**Mars** -- The surface of Mars contains numerous craters, active and extinct volcanoes, and ridges and valleys with extremely deep fractures. Iron oxide found in the dusty soil makes the surface seem rust colored and the skies seem pink in color. The atmosphere is composed of carbon dioxide, nitrogen, argon, oxygen and water vapor. Mars has polar regions with ice caps. Mars has two satellites. Mars was named after the Roman war God.

**Jupiter** – The largest planet in the solar system. Jupiter has 16 moons. The atmosphere is composed of hydrogen, helium, methane and ammonia. There are white colored bands of clouds indicating rising gas and dark-colored bands of clouds indicating descending gases, caused by heat resulting from the energy of Jupiter's core. Jupiter has a Great Red Spot that is thought to be a hurricane type cloud. Jupiter has a strong magnetic field.

**Saturn** -- The second largest planet in the solar system. Saturn has beautiful rings of ice, rock, and dust particles encircling it. Saturn's atmosphere is composed of hydrogen, helium, methane, and ammonia. Saturn has 20-plus satellites around the planet. Saturn was named after the Roman God of agriculture.

**Uranus** -- The second largest planet in the solar system with retrograde revolution. Uranus is a gaseous planet, and it has 10 dark rings and 15 satellites.

Its atmosphere is composed of hydrogen, helium, and methane. Uranus was named after the Greek God of the heavens.

**Neptune** -- Another gaseous planet with an atmosphere consisting of hydrogen, helium, and methane. Neptune has three rings and two satellites. Neptune was named after the Roman Sea God because its atmosphere has the color of the seas.

**Pluto** – Once considered the smallest planet in the solar system, its status as a planet has been reconsidered. It is now considered a planetoid due to its size. Pluto's atmosphere probably contains methane, ammonia, and frozen water. Pluto has one satellite. It revolves around the sun every 250 Earth years. Pluto was named after the Roman God of the Underworld.

### Comets, Asteroids, and Meteors

Astronomers believe that these rocky fragments may have been the remains of the birth of the solar system that never formed into a planet. **Asteroids** are made of rock and found in the region between Mars and Jupiter.

**Comets** are masses of frozen gases, cosmic dust, and small rocky particles. Astronomers think that most comets originate within a dense comet cloud beyond Pluto. Comets consist of a nucleus, a coma, and a tail. A comet's tail always points away from the sun. The most famous comet, **Halley's Comet,** is named after Edmund Halley, the person who first discovered it, in 1758. It returns to the skies near Earth every 75 to 76 years.

**Meteoroids** are composed of particles of rock and metal of various sizes. When a meteoroid travels through Earth's atmosphere, friction causes its surface to heat up and it begins to burn. The burning meteoroid falling through Earth's atmosphere is called a **meteor** (also known as a "shooting star"). **Meteorites** are meteors that strike Earth's surface. A physical example of the impact of the meteorite on Earth's surface can be seen in Arizona. The Barringer Crater is an expansive Meteor Crater. There are plenty of meteor craters found throughout the world.

### SKILL 3.15   Identify structures in the universe (stars, galaxies, quasars) and their characteristics and formation.

Astronomers use groups or patterns of stars called **constellations** as reference points to locate other stars in the sky.  Familiar constellations include: Ursa Major (also known as the Big Bear), and Ursa Minor (known as the Little Bear). Within the Ursa Major, the larger of the two constellations, The Big Dipper is found. Within the Ursa Minor, the smaller of the two constellations, The Little Dipper is found.

Different constellations appear as Earth continues its revolution around the sun with the seasonable changes.

Magnitude stars are 21 of the brightest stars that can be seen from Earth. These are the first stars noticed at night. In the Northern Hemisphere, there are 15 commonly observed first-magnitude stars.

A vast collection of stars is defined as **galaxies**. Galaxies are classified as irregular, elliptical, and spiral. An irregular galaxy has no real structured appearance; most are in their early stages of life. An elliptical galaxy has smooth ellipses (like an oval shape), containing little dust and gas, but composed of an innumerable amount of stars. Spiral galaxies are disk-shaped and have extending arms that rotate around its dense center. Earth's galaxy, found in the Milky Way, is known as a spiral galaxy.

**Terms Related to Deep Space**

A **pulsar** is defined as a variable radio source that emits signals in very short, regular bursts of radio waves and EMR; it is believed to be a rotating neutron star.

A **quasar** is defined as an object that photographs like a star but has an extremely large redshift and a variable energy output; it is believed to be the active core of a very distant galaxy. These have a star-like appearance when viewing them. They also contain black holes.

**Black holes** are defined as an object that has collapsed to such a degree that light cannot escape from its surface; light is trapped by the intense gravitational field.

**SKILL 3.16   Knowledge of hypotheses related to the origin of the solar System.**

Two main hypotheses of the origin of the solar system are: (1) **the tidal hypothesis** and (2) **the condensation hypothesis**.

**The tidal hypothesis** proposes that the solar system began with a near collision of the sun and a large star. Some astronomers believe that as these two stars passed each other, the great gravitational pull of the large star extracted hot gases out of the sun. The mass from the hot gases started to orbit the sun, but then began to cool and condensed into the nine planets. (Few astronomers support this example.)

**The condensation hypothesis** proposes that the solar system began with rotating clouds of dust and gas. Condensation occurred in the center, forming the sun; the smaller parts of the cloud formed the nine planets. (This example is widely accepted by many astronomers.)

Two main theories to explain the origins of the universe include: (1) **The Big Bang Theory** and (2) **The Steady-State Theory.**

The Big Bang Theory has been widely accepted by many astronomers. It states that the universe originated from a magnificent explosion spreading mass, matter and energy into space. The galaxies formed from this material as it cooled during the next half-billion years.

The Steady-State Theory is the least accepted theory. It states that the universe is continuously being renewed. Galaxies move outward and new galaxies replace the older galaxies. Astronomers have not found any evidence to prove this theory.

The future of the universe is hypothesized with the Oscillating Universe Hypothesis. It states that the universe will oscillate or expand and contract. Galaxies will move away from one another and will in time slow down and stop. Gradually, they will move toward each other once again, activating the explosion or The Big Bang theory.

### SKILL 3.17 Identify components of biogeochemical cycles (e.g. carbon, oxygen, hydrogen, and nitrogen) and the order in which they occur.

Essential elements are recycled through an ecosystem. At times, the element needs to be "fixed" in a useable form. Cycles are dependent on plants, algae and bacteria to fix nutrients for use by animals.

**Water cycle** – Almost two percent of all the available water is fixed and held in ice or the bodies of organisms. Available water includes surface water (lakes, ocean, and rivers) and ground water (aquifers, wells). Ninety-six percent of all available water is from ground water. Water is recycled through the processes of evaporation and precipitation. The water present now is the water that has been here since our atmosphere formed.

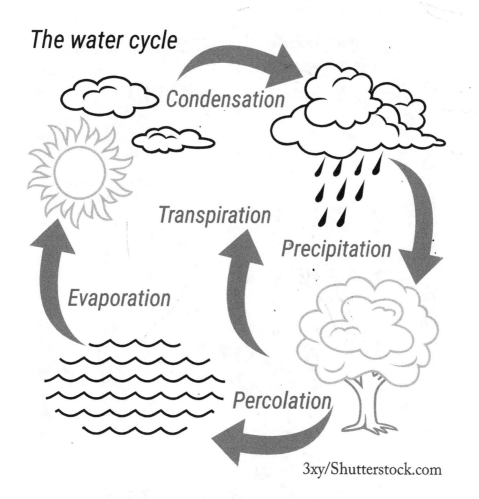

*The water cycle*

Condensation

Transpiration

Precipitation

Evaporation

Percolation

3xy/Shutterstock.com

**Carbon cycle** - Ten percent of all available carbon in the air (from carbon dioxide gas) is fixed by photosynthesis. Plants fix carbon in the form of glucose; animals eat the plants and are able to obtain their source of carbon. When animals release carbon dioxide through respiration, the plants again have a source of carbon to fix.

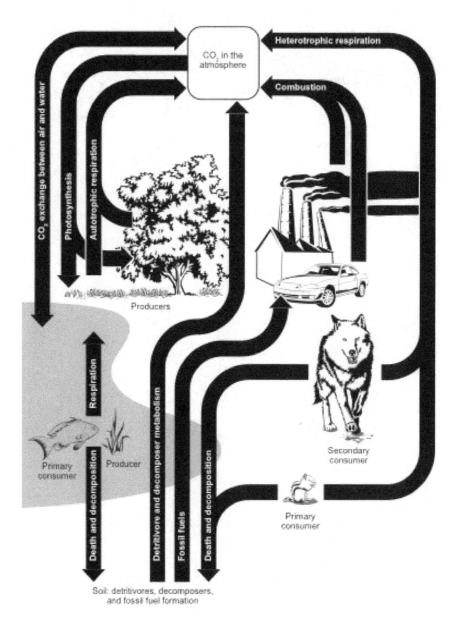

**Nitrogen cycle** – Seventy eight percent of the atmosphere is in the form of nitrogen gas. Nitrogen must be fixed and taken out of the gaseous form to be incorporated into an organism. Only a few genera of bacteria have the correct enzymes to break the triple bond between nitrogen atoms. These bacteria live within the roots of legumes (peas, beans, alfalfa), and add bacteria to the soil so it may be taken up by the plant. Nitrogen is necessary to make amino acids and the nitrogenous bases of DNA.

**Phosphorus cycle** - Phosphorus exists as a mineral and is not found in the atmosphere. Fungi and plant roots have structures called mycorrhizae that are able to fix insoluble phosphates into useable phosphorus. Urine and decayed matter return phosphorus to the earth where it can be fixed in the plant. Phosphorus is needed for the backbone of DNA and for the manufacture of ATP.

**SKILL 3.18    Identify characteristics and composition of air, and atmospheric conditions (e.g. air masses, wind patterns, cloud types, and storms).**

**El Niño** refers to a sequence of changes in the ocean and atmospheric circulation across the Pacific Ocean. The water around the equator is unusually hot every two to seven years. Trade winds normally blowing east to west across the equatorial latitudes, piling warm water into the western Pacific. A huge mass of heavy thunderstorms usually forms in the area and produces vast currents of rising air that displace heat pole-ward. This helps create the strong mid-latitude jet streams. The world's climate patterns are disrupted by this change in location of the massive cluster of thunderstorms. America's west coast experiences a wet winter.

**Air masses** moving toward or away from the Earth's surface are called air currents. Air moving parallel to Earth's surface is called **wind**. Weather conditions are generated by winds and air currents carrying large amounts of heat and moisture from one part of the atmosphere to another. Wind speeds are measured by instruments called anemometers.

The wind belts in each hemisphere consist of convection cells that encircle Earth like belts. There are three major wind belts on Earth: (1) trade winds, (2) prevailing westerly, and (3) polar easterlies. Wind belt formation depends on the differences in air pressures that develop in the doldrums, the horse latitudes, and the polar regions. The Doldrums surround the equator. Within this belt heated air usually rises straight up into Earth's atmosphere. The Horse latitudes are regions of high barometric pressure with calm and light winds and the polar regions contain cold dense air that sinks to the earth's surface.

Winds caused by local temperature changes include sea breezes and land breezes.

**Sea breezes** are caused by the unequal heating of the land and an adjacent, large body of water. Land heats up faster than water. The movement of cool ocean air toward the land is called a sea breeze. Sea breezes usually begin blowing about mid-morning, ending about sunset.

A breeze that blows from the land to the ocean or a large lake is called a **land breeze.**

**Monsoons** are huge wind systems that cover large geographic areas and that reverse direction seasonally. The monsoons of India and Asia are examples of these seasonal winds. They alternate wet and dry seasons. As denser cooler air over the ocean moves inland, a steady seasonal wind called a summer or wet monsoon is produced.

## Cloud Types

**Cirrus clouds** - White and feathery, high in sky clouds

**Cumulus** – Thick, white, fluffy clouds

**Stratus** – Layers of clouds cover most of the sky

**Nimbus** – Heavy, dark clouds that represent thunderstorm clouds

Variation on the clouds mentioned above include **cumulonimbus and stratonimbus**.

The air temperature at which water vapor begins to condense is called the **dew point.**

**Relative humidity** is the actual amount of water vapor in a certain volume of air compared to the maximum amount of water vapor this air could hold at a given temperature.

## Types of Storms

A **thunderstorm** is a brief, local storm produced by the rapid upward movement of warm, moist air within a cumulus-nimbus cloud. Thunderstorms always produce lightning and thunder, accompanied by strong wind gusts and heavy rain or hail.

A severe storm with swirling winds that may reach speeds of hundreds of km per hour is called a **tornado**. Such a storm is also referred to as a "twister." The sky is covered by large cumulonimbus clouds and violent thunderstorms; a funnel-shaped swirling cloud may extend downward from a cumulonimbus cloud and reach the ground. Tornadoes are narrow storms that leave a narrow path of destruction on the ground.

A swirling, funnel-shaped cloud that **extends** downward and touches a body of water is called a **waterspout.**

**Hurricanes** are storms that develop when warm, moist air carried by trade winds rotates around a low-pressure "eye." A large, rotating, low-pressure system accompanied by heavy precipitation and strong winds is called a tropical cyclone or is better known as a hurricane. In the Pacific region, a hurricane is called a typhoon.

Storms that occur only in the winter are known as blizzards or ice storms. A **blizzard** is a storm with strong winds, blowing snow and frigid temperatures. An **ice storm** consists of falling rain that freezes when it strikes the ground, covering everything with a layer of ice.

### SKILL 3.19   Identify the relationship between climate and landforms in both current and geologic time periods.

**Tropical rainforests** covered much of the world millions of years ago. Climatic changes currently limit this biome to about six percent of the Earth's land surface.  Rain forests are found in South America, Africa, New Guinea, Malaysia, Burma, and Indonesia. The moist conditions and constant heat provide for a great growing environment. Fifty percent of all the species in the world are found in the rain forest. Only about one percent of the available sunlight reaches the forest floor. The climate is hot and humid; therefore the landform is a jungle.

**Desert biomes**- Have high temperatures similar to rainforests, but with less moisture. Sand accounts for 15 percent of the desert terrain. Most deserts contain bare rock or pebbles, and gravel areas. The landform requires no moisture.

**Tundra** – Geologic time of the Ice Age has reports of a small number of mankind living there at the poles. The Indians, Aleuts, and Eskimos had little effect on the tundra's ecosystem. The tundra's climate is frigid. Therefore, moss and lichens exist in this fragile environment of polar ice. Scientists are fearful that the polar caps are melting; which not only would change the landform and vegetation at the poles, but also increases water levels worldwide.

**Taiga** – Also known as a boreal forest, has a mild climate that is neither extremely hot nor cold. A taiga also contains several types of lumber including birch, aspen, poplars, and willows. In the niche created by the cool shade of the large trees, there are a great variety of plants. They include mosses, lichens, and ferns. The landform is often laced with rivers and streams. The soils of the taiga thaw out completely each summer and are the home to small invertebrates and vertebrates. These microscopic organisms help break down the leaves and evergreen needles on the forest floor, enriching the soil. The recycled nutrients are then available for use by the taiga's trees so they can continue growing and producing for yet another season.

**Grasslands** – Grasslands have different names in different parts of the world. In North America, they are called prairies; in Asia, steppes; in Africa and

Australia, savannas. Grasses have deep root systems. Therefore the climate would have to be mild to support it. For thousands of years, the growth cycle of the grasslands has created rich topsoil. Farming has converted much of the grasslands into growing crops. Only 11% of the Earth is suitable for farming. Grasses are pollinated by wind. The animals of this region tend to be fast and have mottled colors to blend in with the dry grass.

**SKILL 3.20 Identify the movement of water in the hydrologic cycle, including types of precipitation and forms and causes of condensation.**

Water that falls to Earth in the form of rain and snow is called **precipitation.** Precipitation is part of a continuous process in which water at the Earth's surface evaporates, condenses into clouds, and returns to Earth. This process is termed the **water cycle**. The water located below the surface is called groundwater.

The impact of altitude upon climatic conditions is primarily related to temperature and precipitation. As altitude increases, climatic conditions become increasingly drier and colder. Solar radiation becomes more severe as altitude increases while the effects of convection forces are minimized. Climatic changes as a function of latitude follows a similar pattern. (As a reference, latitude moves either north or south from the equator.) The climate becomes colder and drier as the distance from the equator increases. Proximity to land or water masses produces climatic conditions based upon the available moisture. Dry and arid climates prevail where moisture is scarce; lush tropical climates can prevail where moisture is abundant. Climate, as described above, depends upon the specific combination of conditions making up an area environment. Man has an impact on all environments through activities that produce pollutants in earth, air, and water. It follows then that man is a major player in world climatic conditions.

**SKILL 3.21 Identify ways in which earth and water interact (e.g., soil absorption, run-off, percolation, and sinkholes).**

## Soil Types and Properties

Soils are composed of particles of sand, clay, various minerals, tiny living organisms, and humus, plus the decayed remains of plants and animals.

Soils are divided into three classes according to their texture. These classes are sandy soils, clay soils, and loamy soils.

Sandy soils are gritty and their particles do not bind together firmly. Sandy soils are porous; water passes through them rapidly. Therefore, sandy soils do not hold much water therefore has poor **absorption.**

Clay soils are smooth and greasy; their particles bind together firmly. Clay soils are moist and usually do not allow water to pass through easily. This type of soil has the lowest potential for **run off.**

Loamy soils feel somewhat like velvet and their particles clump together. Loamy soils are made up of sand, clay, and silt. Loamy soils hold water but some water can pass through. **Percolation** (absorption) is best in this type of soil.

**Sinkholes**
A large feature formed by dissolved limestone, which is calcium carbonate, includes sinkholes, caves and caverns. **Sinkholes** are funnel-shaped depressions created by dissolved limestone. Many sinkholes started life as a limestone cavern. Erosion weakens the cavern roof causing it to collapse, forming a sinkhole.

Groundwater usually contains large amounts of dissolved minerals, especially if the water flows through limestone. As groundwater drips through the roof of a cave, gases dissolved in the water can escape into the air. A deposit of calcium carbonate is left behind. Stalactites are icicle-like structures of calcium carbonate that hang from the roofs of caves. Water that falls on a constant spot on the cave floor and evaporates leaves a deposit of calcium carbonate and builds a stalagmite.

**SKILL 3.22 Identify natural and man-made methods of water storage (e.g. aquifers and reservoirs).**

Precipitation that soaks into the ground through small pores or openings becomes groundwater. Gravity causes groundwater to move through interconnected porous rock formations from high to low elevations. The upper surface of the zone saturated with groundwater is the water table. A swamp is an area where the water table is at the surface. When the land dips below the water table, these areas fill with water to form lakes, ponds or streams. Groundwater that flows out from underground onto the surface is called a spring.

Permeable rocks filled with water are called **aquifers**. When a layer of permeable rock is trapped between two layers of impermeable rock, an aquifer is formed. Groundwater fills the pore spaces in the permeable rock. Layers of limestone are common aquifers.

**SKILL 3.23 Identify current problems related to water resources.**

Groundwater provides drinking water for 53% of the population in the United States. Much of the groundwater is clean enough to drink without any type of treatment. Impurities in the water are filtered out by the rocks and soil through which it flows. However, many groundwater sources are becoming contaminated. Septic tanks, broken pipes, agriculture fertilizers, garbage dumps, rainwater runoff, leaking underground tanks, all pollute groundwater. Toxic chemicals from farmland mix with groundwater. Removal of large volumes of groundwater can cause collapse of soil and rock underground, causing the ground to sink. Along shorelines, excessive depletion of underground water supplies allows the intrusion of salt water into the fresh water field. The groundwater supply becomes undrinkable.

### SKILL 3.24 Identify causes and effects of pollutants (e.g., oil spills, acid rain, radioactivity, and ozone).

Pollutants are impurities in air and water that may be harmful to life. Spills from barges carrying large quantities of oil pollute the fish and beaches.

All acids contain hydrogen ions (H+). Acidic substances from factory and car exhausts dissolve in rainwater forming **acid rain.** Acid rain forms predominantly from pollutant oxides in the air (usually nitrogen-based $NO_x$ or sulfur-based $SO_x$), which become hydrated into their acids (nitric or sulfuric acid). When the rain falls onto stone, the acids react with metallic compounds and gradually wear the stone away.

**Radioactivity** is the breaking down of atomic nuclei by releasing particles or electromagnetic radiation. Radioactive nuclei give off radiation in the form of streams of particles or energy. Alpha particles are positively charged particles consisting of two protons and two neutrons. It is the slowest form of radiation. It can be stopped by paper! Beta particles are electrons. It is produced when a neutron in the nucleus breaks up into a proton and an electron. The proton remains inside the nucleus, increasing its atomic number by one. But the electron is given off. They can be stopped by aluminum. Gamma rays are electromagnetic waves with extremely short wavelengths. They have no mass. They have no charge so they are not deflected by an electric field. Gamma rays travel at the speed of light. It takes a thick block of lead to stop them. Uranium is the source of radiation and therefore is radioactive. **Marie Curie** discovered new elements called radium and polonium that actually give off more radiation than uranium.

The major concern with radioactivity is in the case of a nuclear disaster. Medical misuse is also a threat. Radioactivity ionizes the air it travels through. It is strong enough to kill cancer cells or dangerous enough to cause illness or even death. Gamma rays can penetrate the body and damage cells. Protective clothing is needed when working with gamma rays. Electricity from nuclear energy uses the fuel like uranium 235. The devastation of the Russian nuclear power plant disaster (Chernobyl), has evacuated entire regions, as the damage to the land and food source will last for hundreds of years.

## COMPETENCY 4.0      KNOWLEDGE OF LIFE SCIENCE

### SKILL 4.1      Identify the properties of living organisms.

The organization of living systems builds on levels from small to increasingly more large and complex. All aspects, whether it is a cell or an ecosystem, have the same requirements to sustain life. Life is organized from simple to complex in the following way:

> **Organelles** make up **cells,** which make up **tissues,** which make up **organs**. Groups of organs make up **organ systems**. Organ systems work together to provide life for the **organism.**

### SKILL 4.2      Distinguish between living and nonliving things.

Several characteristics have been described to identify living versus non-living substances.

1. **Living things are made of cells**; they grow, are capable of reproduction, and respond to stimuli.

2. **Living things must adapt to environmental changes or perish**.

3. **Living things carry on metabolic processes**. They use and make energy.

### SKILL 4.3      Identify variations in life forms resulting in adaptation to the Environment.

**Charles Darwin** originated the idea of Natural Selection in the mid-1800s. Through the study of finches on the Galapagos Islands, Darwin hypothesized that nature selects the traits that are advantageous to the organism. Those that do not possess the desirable traits die and do not pass on their genes. Those more fit to survive reproduce, thus increasing that gene in the population. Darwin listed four principles to define natural selection:

1. The individuals in a certain species vary from generation to generation.
2. Some of the variations are determined by the genetic makeup of the species.
3. More individuals are produced than will survive.
4. Some traits allow for better survival of an animal.

**Causes of Evolution** - Certain factors increase the chances of variability in a population, thus leading to evolution. Factors that increase variability include mutations, sexual reproduction, immigration, large population, and variation in geographic local. Factors that decrease variation would be natural selection, emigration, small population, and random mating.

**Sexual Selection** – Obviously, the genes that happen to come together determine the makeup of the gene pool. Animals that use mating behaviors may be successful or unsuccessful. An animal that lacks attractive plumage or has a weak mating call will not attract the female, thereby eventually limiting that gene in the gene pool. Mechanical isolation, where sex organs do not fit the female, has an obvious disadvantage.

### SKILL 4.4    Identify cell organelles and their functions.

**Parts of Eukaryotic Cells**

**1. Nucleus** - The brain of the cell. The nucleus contains:

- **Chromosomes**- DNA, RNA and proteins tightly coiled to conserve space while providing a large surface area.
- **Chromatin** - loose structure of chromosomes. Chromosomes are called chromatin when the cell is not dividing.
- **Nucleoli** - where ribosomes are made. These are seen as dark spots in the nucleus.
- **Nuclear Membrane** - contains pores which let RNA out of the nucleus. The nuclear membrane is continuous with the endoplasmic reticulum, which allows the membrane to expand or shrink if needed.

**2. Ribosomes** - the site of protein synthesis. Ribosomes may be free floating in the cytoplasm or attached to the endoplasmic reticulum. There may be up to a half a million ribosomes in a cell, depending on how much protein is made by the cell.

**3. Endoplasmic Reticulum** - These are folded and provide a large surface area. They are the "roadway" of the cell and allow for transport of materials throughout and out of the cell. The lumen of the endoplasmic reticulum helps to keep materials out of the cytoplasm and headed in the right direction. The endoplasmic reticulum is capable of building new membrane material. There are two types:

- **Smooth Endoplasmic Reticulum** - contains no ribosomes on their surfaces
- **Rough Endoplasmic Reticulum** - contain ribosomes on their surfaces. This form of ER is abundant in cells that make many proteins, like in the pancreas, which produces many digestive enzymes.

**4. Golgi Complex or Golgi Apparatus** - This is a stacked structure to increase surface area. The Golgi Complex functions to sort, modify and package molecules that are made in other parts of the cells. These molecules are either sent out of the cell or to other organelles within the cell.

**5. Lysosomes** - found mainly in animal cells. These contain digestive enzymes that break down food, substances not needed, viruses, damaged cell components and eventually the cell itself. It is believed that lysosomes are responsible for the aging process.

**6. Mitochondria** - large organelles that make ATP to supply energy to the cell. Muscle cells have many mitochondria because they use a great deal of energy. The folds inside the mitochondria are called cristae. They provide a large surface area for the reactions of cellular respiration to occur. Mitochondria have their own DNA and are capable of reproducing themselves if a greater demand is made for additional energy. Mitochondria are found in all cells except prokaryotes.

**7. Plastids** - hound in photosynthetic organisms only. They are similar to the mitochondria due to their double membrane structure. They also have their own DNA and can reproduce if the need for the increased capture of sunlight becomes necessary. There are several types of plastids:

- **Chloroplasts** – green; function in photosynthesis. They are capable of trapping sunlight.
- **Chromoplasts** - make and store yellow and orange pigments. They provide color to leaves, flowers and fruits.
- **Amyloplasts** - store starch and are used as a food reserve. They are abundant in roots like potatoes. They do not contain pigment and are found in several plant cells.

**8. Cell Wall** - Found in plant cells only, it is composed of cellulose and fibers. It is thick enough for support and protection, yet porous enough to allow water and dissolved substances to enter. Cell walls are cemented to each other.

**9. Vacuoles** - hold stored food and pigments. Vacuoles are very large in plants. This is allows them to fill with water in order to provide turgor pressure. Lack of turgor pressure causes a plant to wilt.

**10. Cytoskeleton** - composed of protein filaments attached to the plasma membrane and organelles. They provide a framework for the cell and aid in cell movement. They constantly change shape and move about. Three types of fibers make up the cytoskeleton:

- **Microtubules** - largest of the three; make up cilia and flagella for locomotion. Flagella grow from a basal body. Some examples are sperm cells and tracheal cilia. Centrioles are also composed of microtubules.

They form the spindle fibers that pull the cell apart into two cells during cell division. Centrioles are not found in the cells of higher plants.

- **Intermediate Filaments** - They are smaller than microtubules but larger than microfilaments. They help the cell to keep its shape.

- **Microfilaments** - Smallest of the three, they are made of actin and small amounts of myosin (like in muscle cells). They function in cell movement like cytoplasmic streaming, endocytosis and ameboid movement. This structure pinches the two cells apart after cell division, forming two cells.

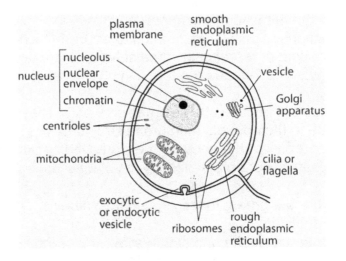

### SKILL 4.5    Identify the sequence of events in mitosis and meiosis and the significance of each process.

The purpose of cell division is to provide growth and repair in body (somatic) cells and to replenish or create sex cells for reproduction. There are two forms of cell division. Mitosis is the division of somatic cells, and **meiosis** is the division of sex cells (eggs and sperm). The table below summarizes the major differences between the two processes.

| MITOSIS | MEIOSIS |
| --- | --- |
| 1. Division of somatic cell. | 1. Division of sex cells. |
| 2. Two cells result from each division. | 2. Four cells or polar bodies result from each division. |
| 3. Chromosome number is identical to parent cells. | 3. Chromosome number is half the number of parent cells. |
| 4. For cell growth and repair. | 4. Recombinations provide genetic diversity. |

## Some Terms to Know:

**Gamete** - sex cell or germ cell; eggs and sperm.
**Chromatin** - loose chromosomes; this state is found when the cell is not dividing.
**Chromosome** - tightly coiled, visible chromatin; this state is found when the cell is dividing.
**Homologues** - chromosomes that contain the same information. They are of the same length and contain the same genes.
**Diploid** - 2n number; diploid chromosomes are a pair of chromosomes (somatic cells).
**Haploid** - 1n number; haploid chromosomes are a half of a pair (sex cells).

## Mitosis

The cell cycle is the life cycle of the cell. It is divided into two stages: **Interphase** and the **mitotic division** where the cell is actively dividing. Interphase is divided into three steps: the G1 (growth) period, where the cell is growing and metabolizing; the S period (synthesis), where new DNA and enzymes are being made; and the G2 phase (growth), where new proteins and organelles are being made to prepare for cell division. The mitotic stage consists of the stages of mitosis and the division of the cytoplasm.

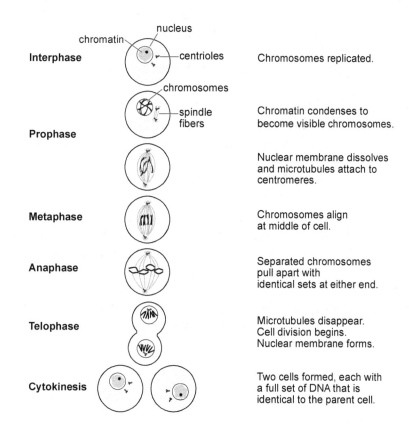

**Interphase** — Chromosomes replicated.

**Prophase** — Chromatin condenses to become visible chromosomes.

Nuclear membrane dissolves and microtubules attach to centromeres.

**Metaphase** — Chromosomes align at middle of cell.

**Anaphase** — Separated chromosomes pull apart with identical sets at either end.

**Telophase** — Microtubules disappear. Cell division begins. Nuclear membrane forms.

**Cytokinesis** — Two cells formed, each with a full set of DNA that is identical to the parent cell.

The stages of mitosis and their events are as follows. Be sure to know the correct order of steps (IPMAT).

1. **Interphase** - Chromatin is loose, chromosomes are replicated, cell metabolism is occurring. Interphase is technically *not* a stage of mitosis.

2. **Prophase** - Once the cell enters prophase, it proceeds through the following steps continuously, with no stopping. The chromatin condenses to become visible chromosomes. The nucleolus disappears and the nuclear membrane breaks apart. Mitotic spindles form, which will eventually pull the chromosomes apart. They are composed of microtubules. The cytoskeleton breaks down and the spindles are pushed to the poles or opposite ends of the cell by the action of centrioles.

3. **Metaphase** - Kinetochore fibers attach to the chromosomes, which cause the chromosomes to line up in the center of the cell (think **m**iddle for **m**etaphase).

4. **Anaphase** - Centromeres split in half and homologous chromosomes separate. The chromosomes are pulled to the poles of the cell, with identical sets at either end.

5. **Telophase** - Two nuclei form with a full set of DNA that is identical to the parent cell. The nucleoli become visible and the nuclear membrane reassembles. A cell plate is visible in plant cells, whereas a cleavage furrow is formed in animal cells. The cell is pinched into two cells. Cytokinesis, or division, of the cytoplasm and organelles occurs.

**Meiosis**- Contains the same five stages as mitosis, but is repeated to reduce the chromosome number by one half. That way, when the sperm and egg join during fertilization, the haploid number is reached. The steps of meiosis are as follows:

**Major function of Meiosis I** - Chromosomes are replicated; cells remain diploid.

**Prophase I** - Replicated chromosomes condense and pair with homologues. This forms a tetrad. Crossing over (the exchange of genetic material between homologues to further increase diversity) occurs during Prophase I.
**Metaphase I** - Homologous sets attach to spindle fibers after lining up in the middle of the cell.
**Anaphase I** - Sister chromatids remain joined and move to the poles of the cell.
**Telophase I** - Two new cells are formed; chromosome number is still diploid.

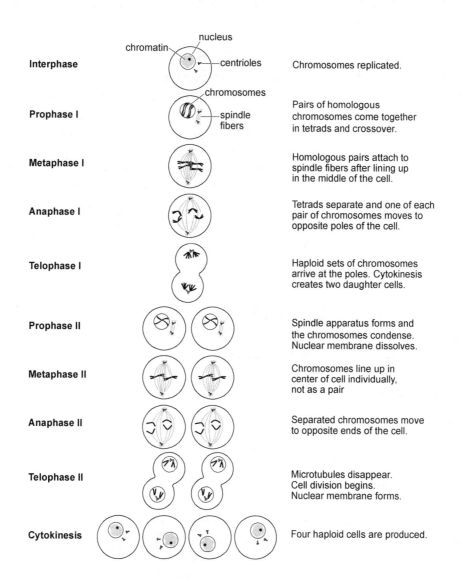

| | | |
|---|---|---|
| **Interphase** | | Chromosomes replicated. |
| **Prophase I** | | Pairs of homologous chromosomes come together in tetrads and crossover. |
| **Metaphase I** | | Homologous pairs attach to spindle fibers after lining up in the middle of the cell. |
| **Anaphase I** | | Tetrads separate and one of each pair of chromosomes moves to opposite poles of the cell. |
| **Telophase I** | | Haploid sets of chromosomes arrive at the poles. Cytokinesis creates two daughter cells. |
| **Prophase II** | | Spindle apparatus forms and the chromosomes condense. Nuclear membrane dissolves. |
| **Metaphase II** | | Chromosomes line up in center of cell individually, not as a pair |
| **Anaphase II** | | Separated chromosomes move to opposite ends of the cell. |
| **Telophase II** | | Microtubules disappear. Cell division begins. Nuclear membrane forms. |
| **Cytokinesis** | | Four haploid cells are produced. |

**Major function of Meiosis II** - To reduce the chromosome number in half.

- **Prophase II** - Chromosomes condense.
- **Metaphase II** - Spindle fibers form again, sister chromatids line up in the center of cell, centromeres divide, and sister chromatids separate.
- **Anaphase II** - Separated chromosomes move to opposite ends of cell.
- **Telophase II** - Four haploid cells form for each original sperm germ cell. One viable egg cell gets all the genetic information and three polar bodies form with no DNA. The nuclear membrane reforms and cytokinesis occurs.

### SKILL 4.6    Identify the consequences of irregularities or interruptions of mitosis and meiosis.

Since it's not a perfect world, mistakes happen. Inheritable changes in DNA are called **mutations**. Mutations may be errors in replication or a spontaneous rearrangement of one or more segments by factors like radioactivity, drugs, or chemicals. The amount of the change is not as critical as where the change is. Mutations may occur on somatic or sex cells. Usually the ones on sex cells are more dangerous since they contain the basis of all information for the developing offspring. Mutations are not always bad. They are the basis of evolution, and if they make a more favorable variation that enhances the organism's survival, then they are beneficial. But, mutations may also lead to abnormalities, birth defects, and even death. There are several types of mutations; let's suppose a normal DNA sequence was as follows:

Normal:    A B C D E F

**Duplication** - One base is repeated.    A B C C D E F

**Inversion** - A segment of the sequence is flipped around.   A E D C B F

**Deletion** - A base is left out.        A B C E F

**Insertion or Translocation** - A segment from another place on the DNA is stuck in the wrong place.        A B C R S D E F

**Breakage** - A piece is lost.        A B C (DEF is lost)

**Nondisjunction** - During meiosis, chromosomes fail to separate properly. One sex cell may get both genes and another may get none. Depending on the chromosomes involved this may or may not be serious. Offspring end up with either an extra chromosome or are missing one. An example of nondisjunction is Down syndrome, where three #21 chromosomes are present.

### SKILL 4.7    Identify cell types, structures and functions.

**Animal cells** – The nucleus is a round body inside the cell. It controls the cell's activities. The nucleus contains threadlike structures called chromosomes. The genes are units found on chromosomes that control cell activities. The cytoplasm has many structures in it. Vacuoles contain the food for the cell. Other vacuoles contain waste materials. Animal cells differ from plant cells because they have centrioles.

**Plant cells** – Plant cells have cell walls. A cell wall differs from cell membranes. The cell membrane is very thin and is a part of the cell. The cell wall is thick and is a nonliving part of the cell. Chloroplasts are other structures not found in animals. They are little bundles of chlorophyll used for photosynthesis. The structure of the cell is often related to the cell's function. Root hair cells differ from leaf epidermal cells. They all have different functions.

**Single cells** – Some single-celled organisms are called **protists.** When you look under a microscope, the animal-like protists are called **protozoans.** They do not have chloroplasts. They are usually classified by the way they move for food. Amoebas engulf other protists by flowing around and over them. The paramecium has a hair like structure allows it to move back and forth like tiny oars searching for food. The euglena is an example of a protozoan that moves with a tail-like structure called flagella.

Plant-like protists have cell walls and grow in the water. **Bacteria** are the simplest microorganisms and belong in Domain Eubacteria. A bacterial cell is surrounded by a cell wall, but there is no nucleus inside the cell. Most bacteria do not contain chlorophyll, so they do not make their own food. The classification of bacteria is by shape. Cocci are round, bacilli are rod-shaped, and spirilli are spiral shaped.

**SKILL 4.8    Apply principles of Mendelian genetics in working monohybrid and dihybrid crosses and crosses involving linked genes.**

**Gregor Mendel** is recognized as the father of genetics. His work in the late 1800s is the basis of our knowledge of genetics. Although unaware of the presence of DNA or genes, Mendel realized there were factors (now known as genes) that were transferred from parents to their offspring. Mendel worked with pea plants and fertilized the plants himself, keeping track of subsequent generations which led to the Mendelian laws of genetics. Mendel found that two "factors" governed each trait, one from each parent. Traits or characteristics came in several forms, known as alleles. For example, the trait of flower color had white alleles and purple alleles. Mendel formed three laws:

**Law of dominance** - In a pair of alleles, one trait may cover up the allele of the other trait. Example:  brown eyes are dominant to blue eyes in humans.

**Law of segregation** - Only one of the two possible alleles from each parent is passed on to the offspring from each parent. (During meiosis, the haploid number ensures that half the sex cells get one allele, half get the other).

**Law of independent assortment** - Alleles sort independently of each other. (Many combinations are possible depending on which sperm ends up with which egg. Compare this to the many combinations of hands possible when dealing a deck of cards).

**Monohybrid Cross** - A cross using only one trait.

**Dihybrid Cross** - A cross using two traits. More combinations are possible.

**Punnet squares** - These are used to show the possible ways that genes combine, or probability of the occurrence of a certain genotype or phenotype. One parent's genes are put at the top of the box and the other parent at the side of the box. Genes combine on the square just like numbers that are added in addition tables we learned in elementary school.

- Example: Monohybrid Cross - four possible gene combinations

- Example: Dihybrid Cross - 16 possible gene combinations

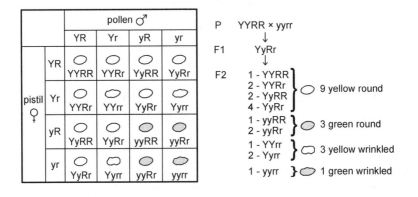

**SKILL 4.9**   **Apply principles of human genetics, including relationships between genotypes and phenotypes and causes and effects of disorders.**

## Some Definitions to Know

**Dominant** - The stronger of the two traits. If a dominant gene is present, it will be expressed. Shown by a capital letter.

**Recessive** - The weaker of the two traits. In order for the recessive gene to be expressed, there must be two recessive genes present. Shown by a lowercase letter.

**Homozygous** – Purebred. Having two of the same genes present; an organism may be homozygous dominant with two dominant genes or homozygous recessive with two recessive genes.

**Heterozygous** - Hybrid. Having one dominant gene and one recessive gene. The dominant gene will be expressed due to the Law of Dominance.

**Genotype** - The genes the organism has. Genes are represented with letters. AA, Bb, and tt are examples of genotypes. When writing a genotype, it is best not to use letter where the upper and lowercase look similar, such as S and s or W and w.

**Phenotype** - How the trait is expressed in an organism. Blue eyes, brown hair, and red flowers are examples of phenotypes.

**Incomplete Dominance** - Neither gene masks the other; a new phenotype is formed. For example, red flowers and white flowers may have equal strength. A heterozygote (Rr) would have pink flowers. If a problem occurs with a third phenotype, incomplete dominance is occurring.

**Codominance** - Genes may form new phenotypes. The ABO blood grouping is an example of co-dominance. A and B are of equal strength and O is recessive. Therefore, type A blood may have the genotypes of AA or AO, type B blood may have the genotypes of BB or BO, type AB blood has the genotype A and B, and type O blood has two recessive O genes.

**Linkage** - genes that are found on the same chromosome usually appear together unless crossing over has occurred in meiosis. (Example: blue eyes and blonde hair).

**Lethal Alleles** - these are usually recessive due to the early death of the offspring. If a 2:1 ratio of alleles is found in offspring, a lethal gene combination is usually the reason. Some examples of lethal alleles include sickle cell anemia, Tay-Sachs and cystic fibrosis. Usually, the coding for an important protein is affected.

**Inborn Errors of Metabolism** - These occur when the protein affected is an enzyme. Examples include PKU (phenylketonuria) and albinism.

**Polygenic Characters** - Many alleles code for a phenotype. There may be as many as twenty genes that code for skin color. This is why there is such a variety of skin tones. Another example is height. A couple of medium height may have very tall offspring.

**Sex-Linked Traits** - The Y chromosome found only in males (XY) carries very little genetic information, whereas the X chromosome found in females (XX) carries very important information. Since men have no second X chromosome to cover up a recessive gene, the recessive trait is expressed more often in men. Women need the recessive gene on both X chromosomes to show the trait. Examples of sex-linked traits include hemophilia and color-blindness.

**Sex-Influenced Traits** - Traits are influenced by the sex hormones. Male pattern baldness is an example of a sex-influenced trait. Testosterone influences the expression of the gene. Mostly men lose their hair due to this.

**SKILL 4.10   Identify the role of DNA and RNA in protein synthesis, translation, transcription, and replication.**

**DNA and DNA Replication**

The modern definition of a gene is that of a unit of genetic information. DNA makes up genes, which in turn make up the chromosomes. DNA is wound tightly around proteins in order to conserve space. The DNA/protein combination makes up the chromosome. DNA controls the synthesis of proteins, thereby controlling the total cell activity. DNA is capable of making copies of itself.

To review the structure of DNA:

1. Made of nucleotides; a five carbon sugar, phosphate group and nitrogen base, (either adenine, guanine, cytosine or thymine).

2. Consists of a sugar/phosphate backbone, which is covalently bonded, meaning they share electrons. The bases are joined down the center of the molecule and are attached by hydrogen bonds, which are easily broken during replication.

3. The amount of adenine equals the amount of thymine, and cytosine equals the amount of guanine.

4. The shape is that of a twisted ladder called a double helix. The sugar/phosphates make up the sides of the ladder and the base pairs make up the rungs of the ladder.

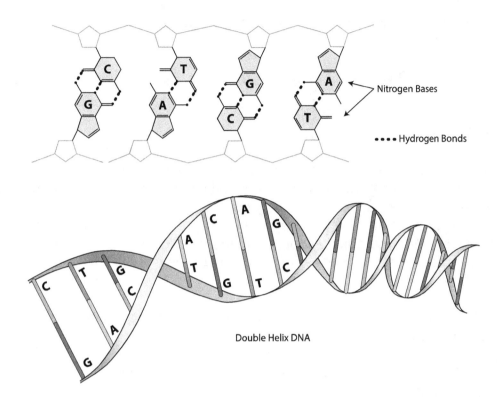

Double Helix DNA

## DNA Replication

Enzymes control each step of the replication of DNA. The molecule untwists. The hydrogen bonds between the bases break and serve as a pattern for replication. Free nucleotides found inside the nucleus join on to form a new strand. Two new pieces of DNA are formed which are identical. This is a very accurate process. There is only one mistake for every billion nucleotides added. This is because there are enzymes (polymerases) present that proofread the molecule. In eukaryotes, replication occurs in many places along the DNA at once. The molecule may open up at many places like a broken zipper. In prokaryotic circular plasmids, replication begins at a point on the plasmid and goes in both directions until it meets itself.

Base pairing rules are important in determining a new strand of DNA sequence. For example, say our original strand of DNA had the sequence as follows:

1. (A T C G G C A A T A G C) - This may be called our sense strand as it contains a sequence that makes sense or codes for something. The complementary strand (or other side of the ladder) would follow base pairing rules (A bonds with T and C bonds with G) and would read as shown below.

2. (T A G C C G T T A T C G)  - When the molecule opens up and nucleotides join on, the base pairing rules create two new identical strands of DNA.

1. A T C G G C A A T A G C          and          A T C G G C A A T A G C
   T A G C C G T T A T C G                        2. T A G C C G T T A T C G

## Protein Synthesis

It is necessary for cells to manufacture new proteins for growth and repair of the organism. Protein Synthesis is the process that allows the DNA code to be read and carried out of the nucleus into the cytoplasm in the form of RNA. This is where the ribosomes are found, which is also where protein synthesis occurs. The protein is then assembled according to the instructions on the DNA. There are several types of RNA. Familiarize yourself with where they are found and their function.

**Messenger RNA** - mRNA copies the code from DNA in the nucleus and takes it to the ribosomes in the cytoplasm.

**Transfer RNA** - tRNA free floats in the cytoplasm. Its job is to carry and position amino acids for assembly on the ribosome.

**Ribosomal RNA** - rRNA is located in the ribosomes. They make a place for the proteins to be made. Much research is being done currently on rRNA to see what other functions it is used for.

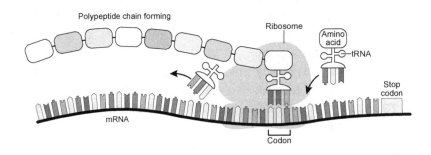

Along with enzymes and amino acids, the RNA's function is to assist in the building of proteins. There are two stages of protein synthesis:

**Transcription** - This phase allows for the assembly of mRNA and occurs in the nucleus where the DNA is found. The DNA splits open and the RNA polymerase reads the code and "transcribes" the sequence onto a single strand of mRNA. For example, if the code on the DNA is: T A C C T C G T A C G A, mRNA will read: A U G G A G C A U G C U. (Remember that uracil replaces thymine in RNA.) Each group of three bases is called a **codon**. The codon will eventually code for a specific amino acid to be carried to the ribosome. "Start" codons begin the building of the protein and "stop" codons end transcription. When the stop codon is reached, the mRNA separates from the DNA and leaves the nucleus for the cytoplasm.

**Translation** - Translation is the assembly of the amino acids to build the protein and occurs in the cytoplasm. The nucleotide sequence is translated to choose the correct amino acid sequence. As the rRNA translates the code at the ribosome, tRNA's which contain an **anticodon** to seek out the correct amino acid and bring it back to the ribosome. For example, using the codon sequence from the example above:

The mRNA reads A U G / G A G / C A U / G C U
The anticodons are UA C / C U C / G U A / C G A (which you would be given and are not expected to memorize). The amino acid sequence would be:

Methionine (start) - Glu - His - Ala.

Be sure to note if the table you are given is written according to the codon sequence or the anticodon sequence, as it will be specified.

The whole process is accomplished through the assistance of **activating enzymes**. Each of the 20 amino acids has their own enzyme. The enzyme binds the amino acid to the tRNA. When the amino acids get close to each other on the ribosome, they bond together using peptide bonds. The start and stop codons are called nonsense codons. There is one start codon (AUG) and three stop codons. (UAA, UGA and UAG) Addition mutations will cause the whole code to shift, thereby producing the wrong protein or at times, no protein at all.

### SKILL 4.11   Distinguish between prokaryotes and eukaryotes

The cell is the basic unit of all living things. There are two types of cells. **Prokaryotic** cells consist only of bacteria and blue-green algae. Bacteria, most likely the first cells, date back in the fossil record to 3.5 billion years ago. The important things that put these cells in their own group are:

1. They have no defined nucleus or nuclear membrane. The DNA and ribosomes float freely within the cell.

2. They have a thick cell wall. This is to protect, give shape, and keep the cell from bursting.

3. The cell walls contain amino sugars (glycoproteins). Penicillin works by disrupting the cell wall, which is bad for the bacteria, but will not harm the host.

4. Some have a capsule made of polysaccharides, which make the bacteria sticky (like on your teeth).

5. Some have pili, which is a protein strand. This also allows for attachment of the bacteria and may be used for sexual reproduction called conjugation.

6. Some bacterial cells have flagella for movement.

**Eukaryotic** cells are found in protists, fungi, plants and animals. Some features of eukaryotic cells include:

1. They are usually larger than prokaryotic cells.

2. They contain many organelles, which are membrane bound areas for specific cell functions.

3. They contain a cytoskeleton, which provides a protein framework for the cell.

4. They contain cytoplasm to support the organelles and contain the ions and molecules necessary for cell function.

**SKILL 4.12  Taxonomy and classification of bacteria, protists, and fungi.**

**Carolus Linnaeus** is termed the father of taxonomy. **Taxonomy** is the science of classification. Linnaeus based his system on morphology (study of structure). Later on, evolutionary relationships (phylogeny) were also used to sort and group species. The modern classification system uses binomial nomenclature. This consists of a two-word name for every species. The genus is the first part of the name and the species is the second part. Notice in the levels explained below that *Homo sapiens* is the scientific name for humans. Starting with the kingdom, the groups get smaller and more alike as one moves down the levels in the classification of humans:

**Kingdom:** Animalia, **Phylum:** Chordata, **Subphylum:** Vertebrata, **Class:** Mammalia, **Order:** Primate, **Family:** Hominidae, **Genus:** Homo, **Species:** sapiens

Species are defined by the ability to successfully reproduce with members of their own kind.

**Kingdom Eubacteria**- Bacteria and blue-green algae, prokaryotic, having no true nucleus, unicellular.

**Kingdom Protista** - Eukaryotic, unicellular, some are photosynthetic, some are consumers.

**Kingdom Fungi** - Eukaryotic, multicellular, absorptive consumers, contain a chitin cell wall.

Bacteria are classified according to their morphology (shape). **Bacilli** are rod shaped bacteria, **cocci** are round bacteria, and **spirili** are spiral shaped. The **Gram stain** is a staining procedure used to identify bacteria. Gram-positive bacteria pick up the stain and turn purple. Gram-negative bacteria do not pick up the stain and are pink in color. Microbiologists use methods of locomotion, reproduction, and the way the organism obtains its food to classify protista.

> **Methods of locomotion** - Flagellates have a flagellum, ciliates have cilia, and amoeboids move through use of pseudopodia.

> **Methods of reproduction** - binary fission is simply dividing in half and is asexual. All new organisms are exact clones of the parent. Sexual modes provide more diversity. Bacteria can reproduce sexually through conjugation, where genetic material is exchanged.

> **Methods of obtaining nutrition** - photosynthetic organisms, or producers, convert sunlight to chemical energy; consumers or

heterotrophs eat other living things. Saprophytes are consumers that live off dead or decaying material.

### SKILL 4.13 Identify helpful and harmful interactions between microbes and humans.

Although bacteria and fungi may cause disease, they are also beneficial for use as medicines and food. Penicillin is derived from a fungus that is capable of destroying the cell wall of bacteria. Most antibiotics work in this way. Viral diseases have been fought through the use of vaccination, where a small amount of the virus is introduced so the immune system is able to recognize it upon later infection. Antibodies are more quickly manufactured when the host has had prior exposure. Viruses are difficult to treat because antibiotics are ineffective against them. That is why doctors do not usually prescribe antibiotics for those who have a cold or the flu—common viral infections.

### SKILL 4.14 Identify the structures and functions of the parts of various types of plants.

**Plant Tissues** - Specialization of tissue enabled plants to get larger. Be familiar with the following tissues and their functions:

**Xylem** - Transports water.

**Phloem** - Transports food (glucose).

**Cortex** - Storage of food and water.

**Epidermis** – Protection. The outermost layer of cells that cover an organism.

**Endodermis** - Controls movement between the cortex and the cell interior.

**Pericycle** - Meristematic tissue that can divide when necessary.

**Pith** - Storage in stems. It is often the spongy tissue in in animals or plants.

**Sclerenchyma and Collenchyma** - Support in stems.

**Stomata** - Openings on the underside of leaves. They let carbon dioxide in and water out (transpiration).

**Guard Cells** - Control the size of the stomata. If the plant has to conserve water, the stomates will close.

**Palisade Mesophyll** - Contain chloroplasts in leaves. Site of photosynthesis.

**Spongy Mesophyll** - Open spaces in the leaf that allow for gas circulation.

**Seed Coat** - Protective covering on a seed.
**Cotyledon** - Small seed leaf that emerges when the seed germinates.

**Endosperm** - Food supply in the seed.

**Apical Meristem** - This is an area of cell division allowing for growth.

**Flowers** - Are the reproductive organs of the plant. Know the following functions and locations:

**Pedicel** - Supports the weight of the flower.

**Receptacle** - Holds the floral organs at the base of the flower.

**Sepals** - Green leaf-like parts that cover the flower prior to blooming.

**Petals** - Contain coloration by pigments to attract insects to assist in pollination.

**Anther** - Male part that produces pollen.

**Filament** - Supports the anther; the filament and anther make up the stamen.

**Stigma** - Female part that holds pollen grains that came from the male part.

**Style** - Tube that leads to the ovary (female).

**Ovary** - Contains the ovules; the stigma, style and ovary make up the carpel.


**SKILL 4.15    Identify the major steps of the plant physiological processes of photosynthesis, transpiration, reproduction and respiration.**

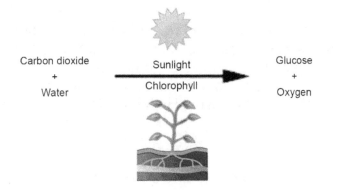

**Photosynthesis** is the process by which plants make carbohydrates from the energy of the sun, carbon dioxide and water. Oxygen is a waste product. Photosynthesis occurs in the chloroplast where the pigment chlorophyll traps sun energy. It is divided into two major steps:

**Light Reactions** - Sunlight is trapped, water is split, and oxygen is given off. ATP is made and hydrogens reduce NADP to $NADPH_2$. The light reactions occur in light. The products of the light reactions enter into the dark reactions (Calvin cycle).

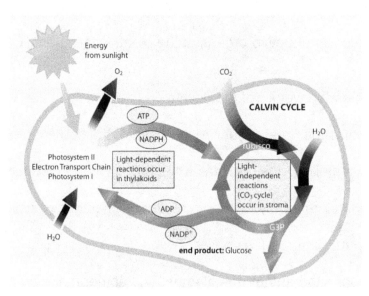

**Dark Reactions** - Carbon dioxide enters during the dark reactions, which can occur with or without the presence of light. The energy transferred from $NADPH_2$ and ATP allow for the fixation of carbon into glucose.

**Cellular Respiration** - During times of decreased light, plants break down the products of photosynthesis through cellular respiration. Glucose, with the help of oxygen, breaks down and produces carbon dioxide and water as wastes. Approximately fifty percent of the products of photosynthesis are used by the plant for energy.

**Transpiration** - Water travels up the xylem of the plant through the process of transpiration. Water sticks to itself (cohesion) and to the walls of the xylem (adhesion). As it evaporates through the stomata of the leaves, the water is pulled up the column from the roots. Environmental factors such as heat and wind increase the rate of transpiration. High humidity will decrease the rate of transpiration.

**Reproduction** - Angiosperms are the largest group in the plant kingdom. They are the flowering plants and produce true seeds for reproduction. They arose about seventy million years ago when the dinosaurs were disappearing. The land was drying up and their ability to produce seeds that could remain dormant until conditions became acceptable and allowed for their success. They also had more advanced vascular tissue and larger leaves for increased photosynthesis. Angiosperms reproduce through a method of **double fertilization**. An ovum is fertilized by two sperm. One sperm produces the new plant, the other forms the food supply for the developing plant.

**Seed dispersal** - Success of plant reproduction involves the seed moving away from the parent plant to decrease competition for space, water and minerals. Seeds may be carried by wind (maples), water (palms), carried by animals (burrs) or ingested by animals and released in their feces in another area.

## SKILL 4.16  Classify the major groups of plants

**Nonvascular Plants** - Small in size, does not require vascular tissue (xylem and phloem) as individual cells were close to their environment. The nonvascular plants have no true leaves, stems or roots.

**Division Bryophyta** - Mosses and liverworts, these plants have a dominant gametophyte generation. They possess rhizoids, which are root-like structures. Moisture in their environment is required for reproduction and absorption.

**Vascular Plants** - The development of vascular tissue enabled these plants to grow in size. Xylem and phloem allowed for the transport of water and minerals up to the top of the plant and food manufactured in the leaves to the bottom of the plant. All vascular plants have a dominant sporophyte generation.

**Division Lycophyta** - Club mosses; these plants reproduce with spores and require water for reproduction.

**Division Sphenophyta** - Horsetails; also reproduce with spores. These plants have small, needle-like leaves and rhizoids. Require moisture for reproduction.

**Division Pterophyta** - ferns; reproduce with spores and flagellated sperm. These plants have true stem and need moisture for reproduction.

**Gymnosperms** - The word means "naked seed." These were the first plants to evolve with the use of seeds for reproduction, which made them less dependent on water to assist in reproduction. Their seeds could travel by wind. Pollen from the male was also easily carried by the wind. Gymnosperms have cones, which protect the seeds.

**Division Cycadophyta** - Cycads; these plants look like palms with cones.

**Division Ghetophyta** - Desert dwellers.

**Division Coniferophyta** - Pines; these plants have needles and cones.

**Division Ginkgophyta** - The Ginkgo is the only member of this division.

**Angiosperms (Division Anthophyta)** - Angiosperms are the largest group in the plant kingdom. They are flowering plants and produce true seeds for reproduction.

**SKILL 4.17   Identify the structures and functions of the organs and systems of various kinds of animals.**

**Skeletal System** - The skeletal system functions in support. Vertebrates have an endoskeleton, with muscles attached to bones. Skeletal proportions are controlled by area to volume relationships. Body size and shape is limited due to the gravitational forces. Surface area is increased to improve efficiency in all organ systems.

**Muscular System** – This system's function is movement. There are three types of muscle tissue. **Skeletal muscle** is voluntary. These muscles are attached to bones. **Smooth muscle** is involuntary. It is found in organs and enable functions such as digestion and respiration. **Cardiac muscle** is a specialized type of smooth muscle.

**Nervous System** - The neuron is the basic unit of the nervous system. It consists of an axon, which carries impulses away from the cell body, the dendrite, which carries impulses toward the cell body and the cell body, which contains the nucleus. **Synapses** are spaces between neurons. Chemicals called neurotransmitters are found close to the synapse. The **myelin sheath**, composed of Schwann cells, covers the neurons and provides insulation.

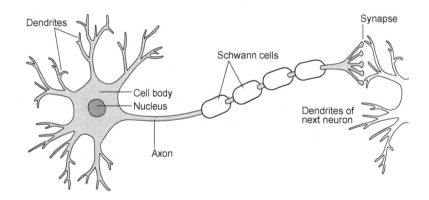

**Digestive System** - The function of the digestive system is to break down food and absorb it into the blood stream where it can be delivered to all cells of the body for use in cellular respiration. As animals evolved, digestive systems changed from simple absorption to a system with a separate mouth and anus, capable of allowing the animal to become independent of a host.

**Respiratory System** - This system functions in the gas exchange of needed oxygen and carbon dioxide waste. It delivers oxygen to the bloodstream and picks up carbon dioxide for release out of the body. Simple animals diffuse gases from and to their environment. Gills allowed aquatic animals to exchange gases in a fluid medium by removing dissolved oxygen from the water. Lungs maintained a fluid environment for gas exchange in terrestrial animals.

**Circulatory System** - The function of the circulatory system is to carry oxygenated blood and nutrients to all cells of the body and return carbon dioxide waste to be expelled from the lungs. Animals evolved from an open system to a closed system with vessels leading to and from the heart.

### SKILL 4.18 Identify the major steps of the physiological process in animals, such as respiration, reproduction, digestion and circulation.

Section 4.23 overlaps with other animals that are mammals.

**Animal** – Respiration takes in oxygen and gives off waste gases. For instance, a fish uses its gills to extract oxygen from the water. Bubbles are evidence that waste gases are expelled. Respiration without oxygen is called anaerobic respiration. Anaerobic respiration in animal cells is also called lactic acid fermentation. The end product is lactic acid.

**Animal reproduction** – Can be asexual or sexual. Geese lay eggs. Animals such as bear cubs, deer, and rabbits are born alive. Some animals reproduce frequently; others do not. Some animals only produce one baby; others produce many.

**Animal digestion** – Some animals only eat meat while others only eat plants. Many animals do both. Nature has created animals with structural adaptations so they may obtain food through sharp teeth or long facial structures. Digestion's purpose is to break down carbohydrates, fats and proteins. Many organs are needed to digest food starting with the mouth. Certain animals, such as birds, have beaks to puncture wood or allow for large fish to be consumed. The tooth structure of a beaver is designed to cut down trees. Tigers are known for their sharp teeth used to rip hides from their prey. Enzymes are catalysts that help speed up chemical reactions by lowering effective activation energy. Enzyme rate is affected by temperature, pH, and the amount of substrate. Saliva contains the enzyme amylase that changes starches into sugars.

**Animal circulation** – The blood temperature of all mammals stays constant regardless of the outside temperature (within reason). This is called warm-blooded, while cold-blooded animals' circulation will vary with the temperature.

## SKILL 4.19   Identify patterns of animal behavior.

**Behavior -** Animal behavior is responsible for courtship leading to mating, communication between species, territoriality and aggression between animals and dominance within a group. Behaviors may include body posture, mating calls, display of feathers or fur, coloration or bearing of teeth and claws.

**Innate behavior -** Behaviors that are inborn or instinctual. An environmental stimulus such as the length of day or temperature results in a behavior. Hibernation among some animals is an innate behavior.

**Learned behavior -** Behavior that is modified due to past experience is called learned behavior.

## SKILL 4.20   Classify the major groups of animals.

**Annelida -** The segmented worms; the first with specialized tissue. The circulatory system is more advanced in these worms and is a closed system with blood vessels. The nephridia are their excretory organs. They are hermaphroditic and each worm fertilizes the other upon mating. Annelids support themselves with a hydrostatic skeleton and have circular and longitudinal muscles for movement.

**Mollusca -** Clams, octopus; the soft-bodied animals. These animals have a muscular foot for movement. They breathe through gills and most are able to make a shell for protection from predators. They have an open circulatory system, with sinuses bathing the body regions.

**Arthropoda -** Insects, crustaceans and spiders; this is the largest group of the animal kingdom. Phylum Arthropoda accounts for about 85% of all the animal species. Animals in the Arthropoda phylum possess an exoskeleton made of chitin. They must molt to grow. Insects, for example, go through four stages of development. They begin as an egg, hatches into a larva, forms a pupa, and then emerges as an adult. Arthropods breathe through gills, tracheae or book lungs. Movement varies, with members being able to swim, fly and crawl. There is a division of labor among the appendages (legs, antennae, etc.). This is an extremely successful phylum, with members occupying diverse habitats.

**Echinodermata** - Sea urchins and starfish; these animals have spiny skin. Their habitat is marine. They have tube feet for locomotion and feeding.

**Chordata** - All animals with a notocord or a backbone. The classes in this phylum include Agnatha (jawless fish), Chondrichthyes (cartilage fish), Osteichthyes (bony fish), Amphibia (frogs and toads; gills which are replaced by lungs during development), Reptilia (snakes, lizards; the first to lay eggs with a protective covering), Aves (birds; warm-blooded with wings consisting of a particular shape and composition designed for flight), and Mammalia (animals with body hair that bear their young alive, possess mammary glands that produce milk, and are warm-blooded).

**SKILL 4.21 Identify the major characteristics and processes of world biomes and communities, including succession, energy flow in food chains and interrelationships of organisms.**

**Ecology** is the study of organisms, where they live and their interactions with the environment. A **population** is a group of the same species in a specific area. A **community** is a group of populations residing in the same area. Communities that are ecologically similar in regards to temperature, rainfall and the species that live there are called **biomes**. Specific biomes include:

**Marine** - Covers 75% of the earth. This biome is organized by the depth of the water. The intertidal zone is from the tide line to the edge of the water. The littoral zone is from the water's edge to the open sea. It includes coral reef habitats and is the most densely populated area of the marine biome. The open sea zone is divided into the epipelagic zone and the pelagic zone. The epipelagic zone receives more sunlight and has a larger number of species. The ocean floor is called the benthic zone and is populated with bottom feeders.

**Tropical Rainforest** - Temperature is constant (25° C), rainfall exceeds 200cm. per year. Located around the area of the equator, the rainforest has abundant, diverse species of plants and animals.

**Savanna** - Temperatures range from 0 – 25° C depending on the location. Rainfall is from 90 - 150cm per year. Plants include shrubs and grasses. The savanna is a transitional biome between the rain forest and the desert.

**Desert** - Temperatures range from 10 – 38° C. Rainfall is under 25cm per year. Plant species include xerophytes and succulents. Lizards, snakes and small mammals are common animals.

**Temperate Deciduous Forest** - Temperature ranges from -24 to 38° C. Rainfall is between 65 and 150cm per year. Deciduous trees are common, as well as deer, bear and squirrels.

**Taiga** - Temperatures range from -24 to 22° C. Rainfall is between 35 and 40cm per year. Taiga is located very north and very south of the equator, getting close to the poles. Plant life includes conifers and plants that can withstand harsh winters. Animals include weasels, mink, and moose.

**Tundra** - Temperatures range from -28 to 15° C. Rainfall is limited, ranging from 10 to 15cm per year. The tundra is located even further north and south of the taiga. Common plants include lichens and mosses. Animals include polar bears and musk ox.

**Polar or Permafrost** - Temperature ranges from -40 to 0° C. It rarely gets above freezing. Rainfall is below 10cm per year. Most water is bound up as ice. Life is limited in these areas.

**Succession** - Succession is an orderly process of replacing a community that has been damaged or has begun where no life previously existed. Primary succession occurs after a community has been totally wiped out by a natural disaster or where life never existed before, as in a flooded area. Secondary succession takes place in communities that were once flourishing but disturbed by some source, either man or nature, but not totally stripped. A climax community is a community that is established and flourishing.

**Definitions of Feeding Relationships**

**Parasitism** - Two species that occupy a similar place; the parasite benefits from the relationship, the host is harmed.

**Commensalism** - Two species that occupy a similar place; neither species is harmed or benefits from the relationship.

**Mutualism (symbiosis)** - Two species that occupy a similar place; both species benefit from the relationship.

**Competition** - Two species that occupy the same habitat or eat the same food are said to be in competition with each other.

**Predation** - Animals that eat other animals are called predators. The animals they feed on are called the prey. Population growth depends upon competition for food, water, shelter and space. The amount of predators determines the amount of prey, which in turn affects the number of predators.

**Carrying Capacity** - This is the total amount of life a habitat can support. Once the habitat runs out of food, water, shelter or space, the carrying capacity decreases and then stabilizes.

**Biogeochemical Cycles** - Essential elements are recycled through an ecosystem. At times, the element needs to be "fixed" in a useable form. Cycles are dependent on plants, algae and bacteria to fix nutrients for use by animals.

**Water Cycle** – Two percent of all the available water is fixed and unavailable in ice or the bodies of organisms. Available water includes surface water (lakes, ocean, and rivers) and ground water (aquifers, wells). Ninety-six percent of all available water is from ground water. Water is recycled through the processes of evaporation and precipitation. The water present now is the water that has been here since our atmosphere formed.

**Carbon Cycle** - Ten percent of all available carbon in the air (from carbon dioxide gas) is fixed by photosynthesis. Plants fix carbon in the form of glucose; animals eat the plants and are able to obtain their source of carbon. When animals release carbon dioxide through respiration, the plants again have a source of carbon to fix again.

**Nitrogen Cycle** - Eighty percent of the atmosphere is in the form of nitrogen gas. Nitrogen must be fixed and taken out of the gaseous form to be incorporated into an organism. Only a few genera of bacteria have the correct enzymes to break the triple bond between nitrogen atoms. These bacteria live within the roots of legumes (peas, beans, alfalfa) and add bacteria to the soil so it may be taken up by the plant. Nitrogen is necessary to make amino acids and the nitrogenous bases of DNA.

**Phosphorus Cycle** - Phosphorus exists as a mineral and is not found in the atmosphere. Fungi and plant roots have a structure called mycorrhizae that are able to fix insoluble phosphates into useable phosphorus. Urine and decayed matter returns phosphorus to the earth where it can be fixed in the plant. Phosphorus is needed for the backbone of DNA and for ATP manufacture.

**Ecological Problems** - Nonrenewable resources are fragile and must be conserved for use in the future. Man's impact on and knowledge of conservation will control our future.

**Biological Magnification** - Chemicals and pesticides accumulate along the food chain. Tertiary consumers have more accumulated toxins than animals at the bottom of the food chain.

**Simplification of the Food Web** - Three major crops feed the world (rice, corn, and wheat). The planting of these foods wipes out other habitats and pushes those animals into other habitats, causing overpopulation or extinction.

**Fuel Sources** - Strip mining and the overuse of oil reserves have depleted these resources. At the current rate of consumption, conservation or alternate fuel sources will guarantee our future as a species.

**Pollution** - Although technology gives us many advances, pollution is a side effect of production. Waste disposal and the burning of fossil fuels have polluted our land, water and air. Global warming and acid rain are two results of the burning of hydrocarbons and sulfur.

**Global Warming** – Rainforest depletion and the use of fossil fuels and aerosols have caused an increase in carbon dioxide production. This leads to a decrease in the amount of oxygen, which is directly proportional to the amount of ozone. As the ozone layer depletes, more heat enters our atmosphere and is trapped. This causes an overall warming effect, which may eventually melt polar ice caps, causing a rise in water levels and changes in climate, which will affect weather systems.

**Endangered Species** - Construction to house our overpopulated world has caused a destruction of habitat for other animals, leading to extinction.

**Overpopulation** - The human race is still growing at an exponential rate. Carrying capacity has not been met due to our ability to use technology to produce more food and housing. Space and water cannot be manufactured and eventually our overuse affects every living thing on this planet.

### SKILL 4.22 Identify the biotic and abiotic factors that influence population density.

**Biotic Factors** - Living things in an ecosystem include plants, animals, bacteria, fungi, etc. If one population in a community increases, it affects the ability of another population to succeed by limiting the available amount of food, water, shelter and space.

**Abiotic Factors** - Non-living aspects of an ecosystem include soil quality, rainfall, and temperature. Changes in climate and soil can cause effects at the beginning of the food chain, thus limiting or accelerating the growth of population.

### SKILL 4.23 Identify the structure and function of organs and systems of the human body.

**Skeletal System** - The skeletal system functions in support. Vertebrates have an endoskeleton, with muscles attached to bones. Skeletal proportions are controlled by area to volume relationships. Body size and shape is limited due to the forces of gravity. Surface area is increased to improve efficiency in all organ systems.

The **axial skeleton** consists of the bones of the skull and vertebrae. The appendicular skeleton consists of the bones of the legs, arms and tail and shoulder girdle. Bone is a connective tissue. Parts of the bone include compact bone which gives strength, spongy bone which contains red marrow to make blood cells, yellow marrow in the center of long bones to store fat cells, and the **periostium** which is the protective covering on the outside of the bone.

A **joint** is defined as a place where two bones meet. Joints enable movement. Ligaments attach bone to bone. **Tendons** attach bones to muscles.

**Muscular System** – Its function is to allow movement. There are three types of muscle tissue. Skeletal muscle is voluntary. These muscles are attached to bones. Smooth muscle is involuntary. It is found in organs and enables functions such as digestion and respiration. Cardiac muscle is a specialized type of smooth muscle and is found in the heart. Muscles can only contract; therefore they work in antagonistic pairs to allow back and forward movement. Muscle fibers are made of groups of myofibrils, which are made of groups of sarcomeres. Actin and myosin are proteins, which make up the sarcomere.

**Physiology of Muscle Contraction** - A nerve impulse strikes a muscle fiber. This causes calcium ions to flood the sarcomere. Calcium ions allow ATP to expend energy. The myosin fibers creep along the actin, causing the muscle to contract. Once the nerve impulse has passed, calcium is pumped out and the contraction ends.

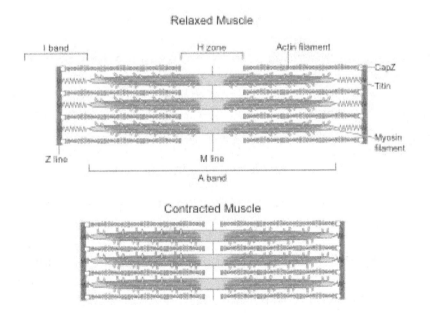

**Nervous System** - The neuron is the basic unit of the nervous system. It consists of an axon, which carries impulses away from the cell body, the dendrite, which carries impulses toward the cell body and the cell body, which contains the nucleus. Synapses are spaces between neurons. Chemicals called neurotransmitters are found close to the synapse. The myelin sheath, composed of Schwann cells, covers the neurons and provides insulation.

**Physiology of the Nerve Impulse** - Nerve action depends on depolarization and an imbalance of electrical charges across the neuron. A polarized nerve has a positive charge outside the neuron. A depolarized nerve has a negative charge outside the neuron. Neurotransmitters turn off the sodium pump, which results in depolarization of the membrane. This wave of depolarization (as it moves from neuron to neuron) carries an electrical impulse. This is actually a wave of opening and closing gates that allows for the flow of ions across the synapse. Nerves have an action potential. There is a threshold of the level of chemicals that must be met or exceeded in order for muscles to respond. This is called the "all or none" response.

The **reflex arc** is the simplest nerve response. The brain is bypassed. When a stimulus (like touching a hot stove) occurs, sensors in the hand send the message directly to the spinal cord. This stimulates motor neurons that contract the muscles to move the hand.

**Voluntary nerve responses** involve the brain. Receptor cells send the message to sensory neurons, which lead to association neurons. The message is taken to the brain. Motor neurons are stimulated and the message is transmitted to effector cells, which cause the end effect.

**Organization of the Nervous System** - The somatic nervous system is controlled consciously. It consists of the central nervous system (brain and spinal cord) and the peripheral nervous system (nerves that extend from the spinal cord to the muscles). The autonomic nervous system is unconsciously controlled by the hypothalamus of the brain. Smooth muscles, the heart and digestion, are controlled by the autonomic nervous system. It works in opposition. The sympathetic nervous system works opposite to the parasympathetic nervous system. For example, if the sympathetic nervous system stimulates an action, the parasympathetic nervous system would end that action.

**Neurotransmitters** - These are chemicals released by exocytosis. Some neurotransmitters stimulate, others inhibit, action.

> **Acetylcholine** - The most common neurotransmitter, it controls muscle contraction and heartbeat. The enzyme acetylcholinesterase breaks it down to end the transmission.

> **Epinephrine** - Responsible for the "fight or flight" reaction. It causes an increase in heart rate and blood flow to prepare the body for action. It is also called adrenaline.

**Endorphins and Enkephalins** - These are natural painkillers and are released during serious injury and childbirth.

**Digestive System** - The function of the digestive system is to break food down and absorb it into the blood stream where it can be delivered to all cells of the body for use in cellular respiration. The teeth and saliva begin digestion by breaking food down into smaller pieces and lubricating it so it can be swallowed. The lips, cheeks and tongue form a bolus or ball of food. It is carried down the pharynx by the process of peristalsis (wave-like contractions) and enters the stomach through the cardiac sphincter, which closes to keep food from going back up. In the stomach, pepsinogen and hydrochloric acid form pepsin, the enzyme that breaks down proteins. The food is broken down further by this chemical action and is churned to for **chyme**. The pyloric sphincter muscle opens to allow the food to enter the small intestine. Most nutrient absorption occurs in the small intestine. Its large surface area, accomplished by its length and protrusions called villi and microvilli allow for a great absorptive surface into the bloodstream. Chyme is neutralized after coming from the acidic stomach to allow the enzymes found there to function. Any food left after the trip through the small intestine enters the large intestine. The large intestine functions to reabsorb water and produce vitamin K. The feces, or remaining waste, are passed out through the anus.

**Accessory Organs** - Although not part of the digestive tract, these organs function in the production of necessary enzymes and bile. The pancreas makes many enzymes to break down food in the small intestine. The liver makes bile, which breaks down and emulsifies fatty acids

**Respiratory System** - This system functions in the gas exchange of needed oxygen and carbon dioxide waste. It delivers oxygen to the bloodstream and picks up carbon dioxide for release out of the body. Air enters the mouth and nose, where it is warmed, moistened and filtered of dust and particles. Cilia in the trachea trap unwanted material in mucus, which can be expelled. The trachea splits into two mainstem bronchial tubes, and the bronchial tubes divide into smaller and smaller bronchioles in the lungs. The internal surface of the lung is composed of alveoli, which are thin-walled air sacs. These allow for a large surface area for gas exchange. The alveoli are lined with capillaries. Oxygen diffuses into the bloodstream and carbon dioxide diffuses out to be exhaled out of the lungs. The oxygenated blood is carried to the heart and delivered to all parts of the body.

The thoracic cavity holds the lungs. A muscle, the diaphragm, below the lungs is an adaptation that makes inhalation possible. As the volume of the thoracic cavity increases, the diaphragm muscle flattens out and inhalation occurs. When the diaphragm relaxes, exhalation occurs.

**Circulatory System** - The function of the circulatory system is to carry oxygenated blood and nutrients to all cells of the body and return carbon dioxide waste to be expelled from the lungs. Be familiar with the parts of the heart and the path blood takes from the heart to the lungs, through the body and back to the heart. In short, deoxygenated blood enters the heart through the inferior and superior vena cava. The first chamber it encounters is the right atrium. It goes through the tricuspid valve to the right ventricle to the pulmonary arteries and then to the lungs where it is oxygenated. It returns to the heart through the pulmonary vein into the left atrium. It travels through the bicuspid valve to the left ventricle where it is pumped to all parts of the body through the aorta.

**Sinoatrial Node (SA node)** - The pacemaker of the heart. Located on the right atrium, it is responsible for contraction of the right and left atrium.

**Atrioventricular Node (AV node)** - Located on the left ventricle, it is responsible for contraction of the ventricles.

**Blood vessels include**:

**Arteries** - Lead away from the heart. All arteries carry oxygenated blood except the pulmonary artery going to the lungs. Arteries are under high pressure.

**Arterioles** - Arteries branch off to form smaller arterioles.

**Capillaries** - Arterioles branch off to form tiny capillaries that reach every cell. Blood moves slowest here due to the small size; only one red blood cell may pass at a time to allow for diffusion of gases into and out of cells. Nutrients are also absorbed by the cells from the capillaries.

**Venules** - Capillaries combine to form larger venules. The vessels are now carrying waste products from the cells.

**Veins** - Venules combine to form larger veins, leading back to the heart. Veins and venules have thinner walls than arteries because they are not under as much pressure. Veins contain valves to prevent the backward flow of blood due to gravity.

**Components of the blood Include**:

**Plasma** – 60% of the blood is plasma. It contains salts called electrolytes, nutrients and waste. It is the liquid part of blood.

**Erythrocytes** - Also called red blood cells. They contain hemoglobin, which carries oxygen molecules.

**Leukocytes** - Also called white blood cells. White blood cells are larger than red cells. They are phagocytic and can engulf invaders. White blood cells are not confined to the blood vessels and can enter the interstitial fluid between cells.

**platelets** - Assist in blood clotting. Platelets are made in the bone marrow.

**Blood Clotting** - The neurotransmitter that initiates blood vessel constriction following an injury is called serotonin. A material called prothrombin is converted to thrombin with the help of thromboplastin. The thrombin is then used to convert fibrinogen to fibrin, which traps red blood cells to form a scab and stop blood flow.

**Immune System:**

**Nonspecific Defense Mechanisms** – They do not target specific pathogens, but are a whole-body response. Results of nonspecific mechanisms are seen as symptoms of an infection. These mechanisms include the skin, mucous membranes and cells of the blood and lymph (i.e.: white blood cells, macrophages). Fever is a result of an increase of white blood cells. Pyrogens are released by white blood cells, which set the body's thermostat to a higher temperature. This inhibits the growth of microorganisms. It also increases metabolism to increase phagocytosis and body repair.

**Specific Defense Mechanisms** - They recognize foreign material and respond by destroying the invader. These mechanisms are specific and diverse. They are able to recognize individual pathogens. They also have recognition of foreign material versus the self. Memory of the invaders provides immunity upon further exposure.

**Antigen** - Any foreign particle that invades the body.

**Antibody** - Manufactured by the body, antibodies recognize and latch onto antigens, hopefully destroying them.

**Immunity** - This is the body's ability to recognize and destroy an antigen before it causes harm. Active immunity develops after recovery from an infectious disease (chicken pox) or after a vaccination (mumps, measles, rubella). Passive immunity may be passed from one individual to another. It is not permanent. A good example would be the immunities passed from a mother to a nursing child.

**Excretory System**

The function of the excretory system is to rid the body of nitrogenous wastes in the form of urea. The functional unit of excretion is the nephron, which make up the kidneys. **Antidiuretic hormone (ADH),** made in the hypothalamus and stored in the pituitary, is released when differences in osmotic balance occur.

This will cause more water to be reabsorbed. As the blood becomes more dilute, ADH release ends.

The **Bowman's capsule** contains the glomerulus, a tightly packed group of capillaries. The glomerulus is under high pressure. Waste and fluids leak out due to pressure. Filtration is not selective in this area. Selective secretion by active and passive transport occur in the proximal convoluted tubule. Unwanted molecules are secreted into the filtrate. Selective secretion also occurs in the loop of Henle. Salt is actively pumped out of the tube and much water is lost due to the hyperosmosity of the inner part (medulla) of the kidney. As the fluid enters the distal convoluted tubule, more water is reabsorbed. Urine forms in the collecting duct, which leads to the ureter then to the bladder where it is stored. Urine is passed from the bladder through the urethra. The amount of water reabsorbed back into the body is dependent upon how much water or fluids an individual has consumed. Urine can be very diluted or very concentrated if dehydration is present.

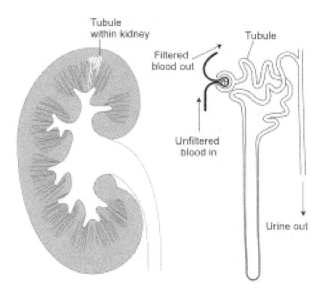

### Endocrine System

The function of the endocrine system is to manufacture proteins called hormones. Hormones are released into the bloodstream and are carried to a target tissue where they stimulate an action. Hormones may build up over time to cause their effect, as in puberty or the menstrual cycle.

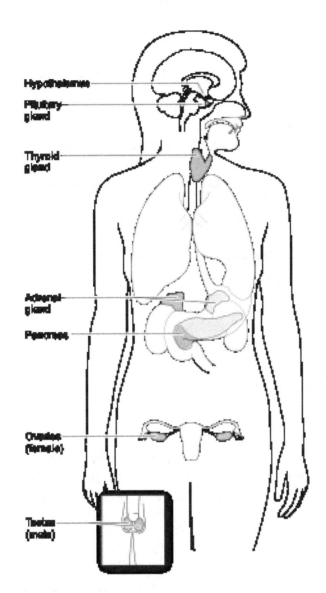

**Hormone activation** - Hormones are specific and fit receptors on the target tissue cell surface. The receptor activates an enzyme, which converts ATP to cyclic AMP. Cyclic AMP (cAMP) is a second messenger from the cell membrane to the nucleus. The genes found in the nucleus turn on or off to cause a specific response.

There are two classes of hormones. **Steroid hormones** come from cholesterol. Steroid hormones cause sexual characteristics and mating behavior. Hormones include estrogen and progesterone in females and testosterone in males. **Peptide hormones** are made in the pituitary, adrenal glands on the kidneys and the pancreas. They include the following:

**Follicle Stimulating Hormone (FSH)** - Production of sperm or egg cells.

**Luteinizing Hormone (LH)** - Functions in ovulation.

**Luteotropic Hormone (LTH)** - Assists in production of progesterone.

**Growth Hormone (GH)** - Stimulates growth.

**Antidiuretic Hormone (ADH)** - Assists in retention of water.

**Oxytocin** - Stimulates labor contractions at birth and let-down of milk.

**Melatonin** - Regulates circadian rhythms and seasonal changes.

**Epinephrine (adrenalin)** - Causes fight-or-flight reaction of the nervous System.

**Thyroxin** - Increases metabolic rate.

**Calcitonin** - Removes calcium from the blood.

**Insulin** - Decreases glucose level in blood.

**Glucagon** - Increases glucose level in blood.

Although you probably won't be tested on individual hormones, be aware that hormones work on a feedback system. The increase or decrease in one hormone may cause the increase or decrease in another. Releasing hormones cause the release of specific hormones.

**Reproductive System**

Sexual reproduction greatly increases diversity due to the many combinations possible through meiosis and fertilization. Gametogenesis is the production of the sperm and egg cells. Spermatogenesis begins at puberty in the male. One spermatozoon produces four sperm. The sperm mature in the seminiferous tubules located in the testes. Oogenesis, the production of egg cells, is usually complete by the birth of a female. Egg cells are not released until menstruation begins at puberty. Meiosis forms one ovum with all the cytoplasm and three polar bodies, which are reabsorbed by the body. The ovum are stored in the ovaries and released each month from puberty to menopause.

**Path of the Sperm** - Sperm are stored in the seminiferous tubules in the testes where they mature. Mature sperm are found in the epididymis located on top of the testes. After ejaculation, the sperm travels up the vas deferens where they mix with semen made in the prostate and seminal vesicles and travel out the urethra.

**Path of the Egg** - Eggs are stored in the ovaries. Ovulation releases the egg into the fallopian tubes, which are ciliated to move the egg along. Fertilization normally occurs in the fallopian tube. If pregnancy does not occur, the egg passes through the uterus and is expelled through the vagina during menstruation. Levels of progesterone and estrogen stimulate menstruation and are affected by the implantation of a fertilized egg so menstruation does not occur.

**Pregnancy** - If fertilization occurs, the zygote implants in about two to three days in the uterus. Implantation promotes secretion of human chorionic gonadotrophin (HCG). This is what is detected in pregnancy tests. The HCG keeps the level of progesterone elevated to maintain the uterine lining in order to feed the developing embryo until the umbilical cord forms. Labor is initiated by oxytocin, which causes labor contractions and dilation of the cervix. Prolactin and oxytocin cause the production of milk.

### SKILL 4.24 Identify the substances that are helpful or harmful in the care and maintenance of the body.

Good nutrition is paramount in maintaining health for growth and development. A balanced diet includes foods from the major food groups of carbohydrates, proteins, lipids and sufficient quantities of vitamins and minerals.

Body pollutants, such as tobacco, drugs and alcohol, interfere with the absorption of nutrients and also may interfere with physical and mental development. They may also damage developing organs, leading to lifelong diseases such as emphysema or asthma.

## COMPETENCY 5.0    KNOWLEDGE OF PHYSICS

### SKILL 5.1    Distinguish between temperature and heat and their measurements.

Heat and temperature are different physical quantities. **Heat** is a measure of energy. **Temperature** is the measure of how hot (or cold) a body is with respect to a standard object.

Two concepts are important in the discussion of temperature changes. Objects are in thermal contact if they can affect each other's temperatures. Set a hot cup of coffee on a desktop. The two objects are in thermal contact with each other and will begin affecting each other's temperatures. The coffee will become cooler and the desktop warmer. Eventually, they will have the same temperature. When this happens, they are in **thermal equilibrium.**

We cannot rely on our sense of touch to determine temperature because the heat from a hand may be conducted more efficiently by certain objects, making them feel colder. **Thermometers** are tools used to measure temperature. A small amount of alcohol in a capillary tube will expand when heated. The thermometer and the object whose temperature it is measuring are put in contact long enough for them to reach thermal equilibrium. Then the temperature can be read from the thermometer scale.

**Three temperature scales are used:**

**Celsius:** The freezing point of water is set at 0 degrees and the steam (boiling) point is 100 degrees. The interval between the two is divided into 100 equal parts called degrees Celsius.

**Fahrenheit:** The freezing point of water is 32 degrees and the boiling point is 212 degrees. The interval between is divided into 180 equal parts called degrees Fahrenheit.

Temperature readings can be converted from one to the other as follows:

| **Fahrenheit to Celsius** | **Celsius to Fahrenheit** |
|---|---|
| $C = 5/9 \, (°F - 32)$ | $F = (9/5)°C + 32$ |

**Kelvin Scale** has the degrees the same size as the Celsius scale, but the zero point is moved to the triple point of water. Water inside a closed vessel is in thermal equilibrium in all three states (ice, water, and vapor) at 273.15 degrees Kelvin. This temperature is equivalent to .01 degrees Celsius. Because the degrees are the same in the two scales, temperature changes are the same in Celsius and Kelvin.

Temperature readings can be converted from Celsius to Kelvin:

| **Celsius to Kelvin** | **Kelvin to Celsius** |
|---|---|
| K = C + 273.15 | C = K - 273.15 |

**Heat** is a measure of energy. If two objects that have different temperatures come into contact with each other, heat flows from the hotter object to the cooler.

**Heat Capacity** of an object is the amount of heat energy that it takes to raise the temperature of the object by one degree.

Heat capacity (C) per unit mass (m) is called **specific heat** (c):

$$c = \frac{C}{m} = \frac{Q/\Delta}{m}$$

Specific heats for many materials have been calculated and can be found in reference tables.

There are a number of ways that heat is measured. In each case, the measurement is dependent upon raising the temperature of a specific amount of water by a specific amount. These conversions of heat energy and work are called the **mechanical equivalent of heat**.

The **calorie** is the amount of energy that it takes to raise one gram of water one degree Celsius. The **kilocalorie** is the amount of energy that it takes to raise one kilogram of water by one degree Celsius. Food calories are kilocalories.

In the International System of Units **(SI),** the calorie is equal to 4.184 **joules**.

**British thermal units (BTU)** - (BTU = 252 calories = 1.054 kJ)

### SKILL 5.2   Identify the types of heat transfer and their characteristics.

Heat energy that is moved into or out of a system is **heat transfer.** The temperature change is positive for a gain in heat energy and negative when heat is removed from the object or system.

The formula for heat transfer is **Q = mcΔT**, where Q is the amount of heat energy transferred, m is the amount of substance (in kilograms), c is the specific heat of the substance, and ΔT is the change in temperature of the substance. It is important to assume that the objects in thermal contact are isolated and insulated from their surroundings. If a substance in a closed container loses heat, then another substance in the container must gain heat.

A **calorimeter** uses the transfer of heat from one substance to another to determine the specific heat of the substance.

When an object undergoes a change of phase, it goes from one physical state (solid, liquid, or gas) to another. For instance, water can go from liquid to solid (freezing) or from liquid to gas (boiling). The heat that is required to change from one state to the other is called **latent heat.**

The **heat of fusion** is the amount of heat that it takes to change from a solid to a liquid or the amount of heat released during the change from liquid to solid. The **heat of vaporization** is the amount of heat that it takes to change from a liquid to a gaseous state.

Heat is transferred in three ways: **conduction, convection, and radiation.**

**Conduction** occurs when heat travels through the heated solid.

The transfer rate is the ratio of the amount of heat per amount of time it takes to transfer heat from an area of an object to another. For example, if you place an iron pan on a flame, the handle will eventually become hot. How fast the handle gets too hot to handle is a function of the amount of heat and how long it is applied. Because the change in time is in the denominator of the function, the shorter the amount of time it takes to heat the handle, the greater the transfer rate.

**Convection** is heat transported by the movement of a heated substance. Warmed air rising from a heat source such as a fire or electric heater is a common example of convection. Convection ovens make use of circulating air to more efficiently cook food. **Radiation** is heat transfer as the result of electromagnetic waves. The sun warms the earth by emitting radiant energy.

An example of all three methods of heat transfer occurs in the thermos bottle or Dewar flask. The bottle is constructed of double walls of Pyrex glass that have a space in between. Air is evacuated from the space between the walls and the inner wall is silvered. The lack of air between the walls lessens heat loss by convection and conduction. The heat inside is reflected by the silver, cutting down heat transfer by radiation. Hot liquids remain hotter and cold liquids remain colder longer.

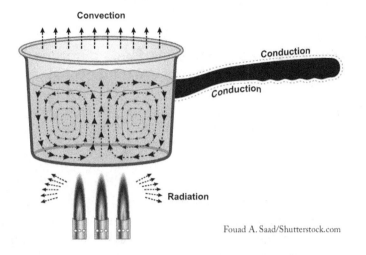

Fouad A. Saad/Shutterstock.com

**SKILL 5.3  Identify the laws of thermodynamics and the related concepts of molecular motion and thermal expansion.**

The relationship between heat and forms of energy and work (mechanical, electrical, etc.) are the **Laws of Thermodynamics.** These laws deal strictly with systems in thermal equilibrium and not those with in the process of rapid change or in a state of transition. Systems that are nearly always in a state of equilibrium are called **reversible systems.**

**The first law of thermodynamics** is a restatement of conservation of energy. The change in heat energy supplied to a system (Q) is equal to the sum of the change in the internal energy (U) and the change in the work done by the system against internal forces (W). It can be represented as $\Delta Q = \Delta U + \Delta W$.

**The second law of thermodynamics** is stated in two parts:

1. No machine is 100% efficient. It is impossible to construct a machine that only absorbs heat from a heat source and performs an equal amount of work because some heat will always be lost to the environment.

2. Heat cannot spontaneously pass from a colder to a hotter object. An ice cube sitting on a hot sidewalk will melt into a little puddle, but it will never spontaneously cool and form the same ice cube. Certain events have a preferred direction called the **arrow of time.**

**Entropy** is the measure of how much energy or heat is available for work. Work occurs only when heat is transferred from hot to cooler objects. Once this is done, no more work can be extracted from them alone. The energy is still being conserved, but is not available for work as long as the objects are the same temperature. Theory has it that, eventually, all things in the universe will reach the same temperature. If this happens, energy will no longer be usable.

### SKILL 5.4  Identify the types and characteristics of forces, examples of Newton's laws of motion and the methods of measuring them.

**Dynamics** is the study of the relationship between motion and the forces affecting motion. **Force** causes motion.

Mass and weight are not the same quantities. An object's **mass** gives it a reluctance to change its current state of motion. It is also the measure of an object's resistance to acceleration. The force that the earth's gravity exerts on an object with a specific mass is called the object's weight on earth. Weight is a force that is measured in Newtons (N). Weight (W) = mass x acceleration due to gravity. (**W = mg**). To illustrate the difference between mass and weight, picture two rocks of equal mass on a balance scale. If the scale is balanced in one place, it will be balanced everywhere, regardless of the gravitational field. However, the weight of the stones would vary on a spring scale, depending upon the gravitational field. In other words, the stones would be balanced both on Earth and on the Moon. However, the weight of the stones would be greater on Earth than on the Moon.

**Newton's Laws of Motion:**

**Newton's First Law of Motion** is also called the Law of Inertia. It states that an object at rest will remain at rest and an object in motion will remain in motion at a constant velocity unless acted upon by an external force.

**Newton's Second Law of Motion** states that if a net force acts on an object, it will cause the acceleration of the object. The relationship between force and motion is Force equals mass times acceleration. (**F = ma**).

**Newton's Third Law** states that for every action there is an equal and opposite reaction. Therefore, if an object exerts a force on another object, that second object exerts an equal and opposite force on the first.

Surfaces that touch each other have a certain resistance to motion. This resistance is **friction.**

1. The materials that make up the surfaces will determine the magnitude of the frictional force.
2. The frictional force is independent of the area of contact between the two surfaces.
3. The direction of the frictional force is opposite to the direction of motion.

4. The frictional force is proportional to the normal force between the two surfaces in contact.

**Static friction** describes the force of friction of two surfaces that are in contact but do not have any motion relative to each other, such as a block sitting on an inclined plane. **Kinetic friction** describes the force of friction of two surfaces in contact with each other when there is relative motion between the surfaces.

When an object moves in a circular path, a force must be directed toward the center of the circle in order to keep the motion going. This constraining force is called **centripetal force**. Gravity is the centripetal force that keeps a satellite circling the earth.

### SKILL 5.5   Apply knowledge of forces and motion to solve problems.

Use Skill 5.5 along with any physics classes or kinesiology classes to solve problems regarding buoyancy, centripetal force, elastic force, electric force, force on moving objects, muscular force, force on objects at rest, gravitational, simple machines and force, and work and force.

**Push and Pulls** – Pushing a volleyball or pulling a bowstring applies muscular force when the muscles expand and contract. When the bowstring is released, it creates elastic force and any object will return to its original shape.

**Rubbing** – Friction opposes the motion of one surface past another. Friction is common when slowing down a car.

**Pull of Gravity** – This is a force of attraction between two objects. Gravity questions can be raised in discussions about the earth, as well as about other planets and the black hole.

**Forces on Objects at Rest** – The formula F=ma means that a force equals mass over acceleration. An object will not move unless the force is strong enough to move the mass. Also there can be opposing forces holding the object in place. For instance, a boat may want to be forced by the currents to drift away but an equal and opposite force is a rope holding it to a dock.

**Forces on a Moving Object** – Overcoming inertia is the tendency of any object to oppose a change in motion. An object at rest tends to stay at rest. An object that is moving tends to keep moving.

**Inertia and Circular Motion** – The centripetal force is provided by the high banking of the curved road and by friction between the wheels and the road. This inward force, which keeps an object moving in a circle, is centripetal force.

**SKILL 5.6    Identify simple machines.**

1.  Inclined plane – One example is a ramp.
2.  Lever – A bar used for prying or dislodging something.
3.  Wheel and axle – The axle is the shaft that the wheel revolves around.
4.  Pulley - A grooved wheel turned by a cord or chain.


**SKILL 5.7   Apply knowledge of simple machines to solve problems
             involving work, power, mechanical advantage, and efficiency.**

**Work and Energy:**

**Work** is done on an object when an applied force moves through a distance.

**Power** is the work done divided by the amount of time that it took to do it.
(Power = Work / time)


**SKILL 5.8   Identify the process by which sound is produced and
             transmitted.**

Sound waves are produced by a vibrating body. The vibrating object moves
forward and compresses the air in front of it, then reverses direction so that the
pressure on the air is lessened and expansion of the air molecules occurs. One
compression and expansion creates one longitudinal wave. Sound can be
transmitted through any gas, liquid, or solid. However, it cannot be transmitted
through a vacuum because there are no particles present to vibrate and bump
into their adjacent particles to transmit the waves.

The vibrating air molecules move back and forth, parallel to the direction of
motion of the wave, as they pass the energy from adjacent air molecules closer
to the source to air molecules farther away from the source.


**SKILL 5.9   Identify the characteristics of the components of a sound wave
             and methods for their measurements.**

The **pitch** of a sound depends on the **frequency** that the ear receives. High-
pitched sound waves have high frequencies. High notes are produced by an
object that is vibrating at a greater number of times per second than one that
produces a low note.

The **intensity** of a sound is the amount of energy that crosses a unit of area in a
given unit of time. The loudness of the sound is subjective and depends upon the
effect on the human ear. Two tones of the same intensity but different pitches

may appear to have different loudness. The intensity level of sound is measured in decibels. Normal conversation is about 60 decibels. A power saw is about 110 decibels.

The **amplitude** of a sound wave determines its loudness. Loud sound waves have large amplitudes. The larger the sound wave, the more energy is needed to create the wave.

An oscilloscope is useful in studying waves because it gives a picture of the wave that shows the crest and trough of the waves. **Interference** is the interaction of two or more waves that meet. If the waves interfere constructively, the crest of each one meets the crests of the others. They combine into a crest with greater amplitude. As a result, you hear a louder sound. If the waves interfere destructively, then the crest of one meets the trough of another. They produce a wave with lower amplitude that produces a softer sound.

If you have two tuning forks that produce different pitches, then one will produce sounds of a slightly higher frequency. When you strike the two forks simultaneously, you may hear beats. **Beats** are a series of loud and soft sounds. This is because when the waves meet, the crests combine at some points and produce loud sounds. At other points, they nearly cancel each other out and produce soft sounds.

### SKILL 5.10 Apply the characteristics of sound as they apply to everyday situations (e.g. music, noise, and the Doppler Effect).

When a piano tuner tunes a piano, he only uses one tuning fork, even though there are many strings on the piano. He adjusts to first string to be the same as that of the tuning fork. Then he listens to the beats that occur when both the tuned and untuned strings are struck. He adjusts the untuned string until he can hear the correct number of beats per second. This process of striking the untuned and tuned strings together and timing the beats is repeated until all the piano strings are tuned.

Pleasant sounds have a regular wave pattern that is repeated over and over. Sounds that have an irregular that do not happen with regularity are unpleasant and are called **noise**.

Change in experienced frequency due to relative motion of the source of the sound is called the **Doppler Effect.** When a siren approaches, the pitch is high. When it passes, the pitch drops. As a moving sound source approaches a listener, the sound waves are closer together, causing an increase in frequency in the sound that is heard. As the source passes the listener, the waves spread out and the frequency experienced by the listener is lower.

### SKILL 5.11 Identify the principles relating to the changing pathways of light.

Shadows illustrate one of the basic properties of light. Light travels in a straight line. If you put your hand between a light source and a wall, you will interrupt the light and produce a shadow.

When light hits a surface, it is **reflected.** The angle of the incoming light—the angle of incidence—is the same as the angle of the reflected light, the angle of reflection. It is this reflected light that allows you to see objects. You see the objects when the reflected light reaches your eyes.

Different surfaces reflect light differently. Rough surfaces scatter light in many different directions. A smooth surface reflects the light in one direction. If it is smooth and shiny (like a mirror), reflection allows you to see your image in the surface.

When light enters a different medium, it bends. This bending or change of speed is called **refraction**.

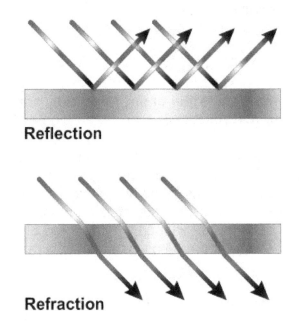

**Reflection**

**Refraction**

Fouad A. Saad/Shutterstock.com

Light can be **diffracted**, or bent around the edges of an object. Diffraction occurs when light goes through a narrow slit. As light passes through it, the light bends slightly around the edges of the slit. You can demonstrate this by pressing your thumb and forefinger together, making a very thin slit between them. Hold them about 8 cm from your eye and look at a distant source of light. The pattern you observe is caused by the diffraction of light.

**SKILL 5.12 Apply knowledge of light and optics to practical applications, such as eyeglasses, other optical instruments, and communication.**

Light and other electromagnetic radiation can be polarized because the waves are transverse. The distinguishing characteristic of transverse waves is that they are perpendicular to the direction of the motion of the wave. Polarized light has vibrations confined to a single plane that is perpendicular to the direction of motion. Light can be polarized by passing it through special filters that block all vibrations except those in a single plane. By blocking out all but one place of vibration, polarized sunglasses cut down on glare.

Light can travel through thin fibers of glass or plastic without escaping the sides. Light on the inside of these fibers is reflected so that it stays inside the fiber until it reaches the other end. Such fiber optics are being used to carry telephone messages. Sound waves are converted to electric signals, which are coded into a series of light pulses, which move through the optical fiber until they reach the other end. At that time, they are converted back into sound.

A curved mirror, opposed to a flat one, can produce a real image. A real image is produced when light passes through the point where the image appears. A real image can be projected onto a screen. Cameras use a convex lens to produce an image on the film. A **convex lens** is thicker in the middle than at the edges. The image size depends upon the focal length (distance from the focus to the lens). The longer the focal length, the larger the image. A **converging lens** produces a real image whenever the object is far enough from the lens that the rays of light from the object can hit the lens and be focused into a real image on the other side of the lens.

Eyeglasses can help correct sight defects by changing where the image seen is focused on the retina of the eye. If a person is nearsighted, the lens of his or her eye focuses images in front of the retina. In this case, the corrective lens placed in the eyeglasses will be concave so that the image will reach the retina. In the case of farsightedness, the lens of the eye focuses the image behind the retina. The correction will call for a convex lens to be fitted into the glass frames so that the image is brought forward into sharper focus.

**SKILL 5.13 Identify the parts of the electromagnetic spectrum and the relative wavelengths and energy associated with each.**

The electromagnetic spectrum is measured in frequency (f), in hertz, and wavelength ($\lambda$), in meters. The frequency times the wavelength of every electromagnetic wave equals the speed of light ($3.0 \times 10^8$ meters/second).

Roughly, the range of wavelengths of the electromagnetic spectrum are:

| | $\underline{f}$ | | $\lambda$ | |
|---|---|---|---|---|
| Radio waves | $10^{5}$- $10^{-1}$ meters | | $10^{3}$ -$10^{9}$ | hertz |
| Microwaves | $10^{-1}$ - $10^{-3}$ meters | | $10^{9}$ -$10^{11}$ | hertz |
| Infrared radiation | $10^{-3}$ - $10^{-6}$ meters | | $10^{11.2}$-$10^{14.3}$ | hertz |
| Visible light | $10^{-6.2}$ $10^{-6.9}$ meters | | $10^{14.3}$-$10^{15}$ | hertz |
| Ultraviolet radiation | $10^{-7}$ - $10^{-9}$ meters | | $10^{15}$ -$10^{17.2}$ | hertz |
| X-Rays | $10^{-9}$ - $10^{-11}$ meters | | $10^{17.2}$ -$10^{19}$ | hertz |
| Gamma Rays | $10^{-11}$- $10^{-15}$ meters | | $10^{19}$ - $10^{23.25}$ | hertz |

### SKILL 5.14  Identify characteristics and examples of static electricity and charged objects.

Electrostatics is the study of stationary electric charges. A plastic rod that is rubbed with fur or a glass rod that is rubbed with silk will become electrically charged and will attract small pieces of paper. The charge on the plastic rod rubbed with fur is negative and the charge on glass rod rubbed with silk is positive.

**Electrically charged** objects share these characteristics:

1. Like charges repel one another.
2. Opposite charges attract each other.
3. Charge is conserved. A neutral object has no net change. If the plastic rod and fur are initially neutral and when the rod becomes charged by the fur, a negative charge is transferred from the fur to the rod. The net negative charge on the rod is equal to the net positive charge on the fur.

Materials through which electric charges can easily flow are called conductors. On the other hand, an **insulator** is a material through which electric charges do not move easily, if at all. A simple device used to indicate the existence of a positive or negative charge is called an **electroscope**. An electroscope is made up of a conducting knob and attached very lightweight conducting leaves, usually made of gold foil or aluminum foil. When a charged object touches the knob, the leaves push away from each other because like charges repel. It is not possible to tell whether or not the charge is positive or negative.

### Charging by Induction:

Touch the knob with a finger while a charged rod is nearby. The electrons will be repulsed and flow out of the electroscope through the hand. If the hand is removed while the charged rod remains close, the electroscope will retain the charge.

When an object is rubbed with a charged rod, the object will take on the same charge as the rod. However, charging by induction gives the object the opposite charge as that of the charged rod.

**Grounding Charge:**

Charge can be removed from an object by connecting it to the earth through a conductor. The removal of static electricity by conduction is called **grounding**.

**SKILL 5.15  Identify types, characteristics, and methods of measuring current and circuits.**

An **electric circuit** is a path along which electrons flow. A simple circuit can be created with a dry cell, wire, and a bell, or light bulb. When all are connected, the electrons flow from the negative terminal, through the wire to the device and back to the positive terminal of the dry cell. If there are no breaks in the circuit, the device will work. The circuit is closed. Any break in the flow will create an open circuit and cause the device to shut off.

The device (bell, bulb) is an example of a **load**. A load is a device that uses energy. Suppose you also add a buzzer so that the bell rings when you press the buzzer button. The buzzer is acting as a **switch**. A switch is a device that opens or closes a circuit. Pressing the buzzer makes the connection complete and the bell rings. When the buzzer is not engaged, the circuit is open and the bell is silent.

A **series circuit** is one where the electrons have only one path along which they can move. When one load in a series circuit goes out, the circuit is open. An example of this is a set of Christmas tree lights that is missing a bulb. None of the bulbs will work.

A **parallel circuit** is one where the electrons have more than one path to move along. Each path is known as a path. If a load goes out in a parallel circuit, the other load will still work because the electrons can still find a way to continue moving along the path.

When an electron goes through a load, it does work and therefore loses some of its energy. The measure of how much energy is lost is called the **potential difference**. The potential difference between two points is the work needed to move a charge from one point to another.

Potential difference is measured in a unit called the volt. **Voltage** is potential difference. The higher the voltage, the more energy the electrons have. This energy is measured by a device called a voltmeter. To use a voltmeter, place it in a circuit parallel with the load you are measuring.

**Current** is the number of electrons per second that flow past a point in a circuit. Current is measured with a device called an ammeter. To use an ammeter, put it in series with the load you are measuring.

As electrons flow through a wire, they lose potential energy. Some is changed into heat energy because of resistance. **Resistance** is the ability of the material to oppose the flow of electrons through it. All substances have some resistance, even if they are a good conductor such as copper. This resistance is measured in units called **ohms**. A thin wire will have more resistance than a thick one because it will have less room for electrons to travel. In a thicker wire, there will be more possible paths for the electrons to flow. Resistance also depends upon the length of the wire. The longer the wire, the more resistance it will have. Potential difference, resistance, and current form a relationship know as **Ohm's Law**. Current **(I)** is equal to potential difference **(V)** divided by resistance **(R)**.

$$I = V / R$$

If you have a wire with resistance of 5 ohms and a potential difference of 75 volts, you can calculate the current by:

**I = 75 volts / 5 ohms**
**I = 15 amperes**

A current of 10 or more amperes will cause a wire to get hot. Twenty-two amperes is about the maximum for a house circuit. Anything above 25 amperes can start a fire.

### SKILL 5.16 Apply knowledge of currents, circuits, conductors, insulators, and resistors to everyday situations.

Electricity can be used to change the chemical composition of a material. For instance, when electricity is passed through water, it breaks the water down into hydrogen gas and oxygen gas.

Circuit breakers in a home monitor the electric current. If there is an overload, the circuit breaker will create an open circuit, stopping the flow of electricity.

Computers can be made small enough to fit inside a plastic credit card by creating what is known as a solid-state device. In this device, electrons flow through solid material such as silicon.

Resistors are used to regulate volume on a television or radio or through a dimmer switch for lights.

A bird can sit on an electrical wire without being electrocuted because the bird and the wire have about the same potential. However, if that same bird would touch two wires at the same time it would not have to worry about flying south next year.

When caught in an electrical storm, a car is a relatively safe place from lightening because of the resistance of the rubber tires. A metal building would not be safe unless there was a lightning rod that would attract the lightening and conduct it to the ground.

### SKILL 5.17  Identify characteristics of types of magnets, magnetic fields, and compasses.

Magnets have a north pole and a south pole. Like poles repel and different poles attract. A **magnetic field** is the space around a magnet where its force will affect objects. The closer you are to a magnet, the stronger the force. As you move away, the force becomes weaker.

Some materials act as magnets and some do not. This is because magnetism is a result of electrons in motion. The most important motion in this case is the spinning of the individual electrons. Electrons spin in pairs in opposite directions in most atoms. Each spinning electron creates a magnetic field that is canceled out by the electron that is spinning in the opposite direction.

In an atom of iron, there are four unpaired electrons. The magnetic fields of these are not canceled out. Their fields add up to make a tiny magnet. Their fields exert forces on each other setting up small areas in the iron called **magnetic domains**, where atomic magnetic fields line up in the same direction.

You can make a magnet out of an iron nail by stroking the nail in the same direction repeatedly with a magnet. This causes poles in the atomic magnets in the nail to be attracted to the magnet. The tiny magnetic fields in the nail line up in the direction of the magnet. The magnet causes the domains pointing in its direction in the nail to grow. Eventually, one large domain results and the nail becomes a magnet.

A bar magnet has a north pole and a south pole. If you break the magnet in half, each piece will have a north and south pole. This is called the **magnetic domain**. When the magnet is broken, the atoms realign themselves to the electrical charges of each pole remain the same.

The Earth has a magnetic field. In a compass, a tiny, lightweight magnet is suspended and will align its south pole up with Earth's North Pole. A magnet can be made out of a coil of wire by connecting the ends of the coil to a battery.

When the current goes through the wire, the wire acts in the same way that a magnet does; it is called an **electromagnet**.

The poles of the electromagnet will depend upon which way the electric current runs. An electromagnet can be made more powerful in three ways:

1. create more coils
2. insert an iron core (nail) inside the coils
3. use more battery power

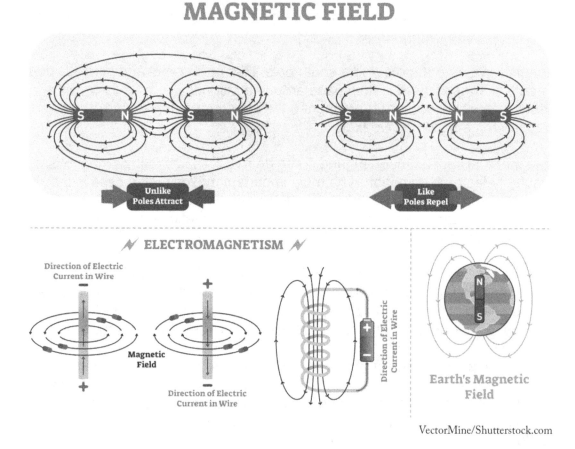

VectorMine/Shutterstock.com

**SKILL 5.18   Apply knowledge of magnets and magnetic fields to everyday situations**

Telegraphs use electromagnets to work. When a telegraph key is pushed, current flows through a circuit, turning on an electromagnet, which attracts an iron bar. The iron bar hits a sounding board, which responds with a click. Release the key and the electromagnet turns off. Messages can be sent around the world in this way.

Scrap metal can be removed from waste materials by the use of a large electromagnet that is suspended from a crane. When the electromagnet is turned on, the metal in the pile of waste will be attracted to it. All other materials will stay on the ground.

Air conditioners, vacuum cleaners, and washing machines use electric motors. An electric motor uses an electromagnet to change electric energy into mechanical energy.

### SKILL 5.19 Distinguish between fission and fusion and the resulting radioactivity.

Chemical reactions involve the breaking and forming of bonds between atoms. Bonds involve only the outer electrons and do not affect the nucleus. When a reaction involves a nucleus, elements are changed into different elements. This is called a **nuclear reaction**. The binding energy is released when the nuclei of atoms are split apart in a nuclear reaction. This binding energy is called **nuclear energy**.

There are two types of nuclear reactions:

**Nuclear fission** occurs when the nuclei are split apart. Smaller nuclei are formed and energy is released. The fission of many atoms in a short time period releases a large amount of energy. "Heavy water" is used in a nuclear reactor to slow down neutrons, controlling and moderating the nuclear reactions. Controlling the release so that energy is released slowly gives us nuclear submarines and nuclear power plants.

**Nuclear fusion** is the opposite as it occurs when small nuclei combine to form a larger nucleus. It begins with the hydrogen atom, which has the smallest nuclei. During one type of fusion, four hydrogen nuclei are fused at very high pressures and temperatures. They form one helium atom. The sun and stars are examples of fusion. They are made mostly of hydrogen that is constantly fusing. As the hydrogen forms helium, it releases an energy that we see as light. When all of the hydrogen is used, the star will no longer shine. Scientists estimate that the sun has enough hydrogen to keep it glowing for another four billion years.

During a nuclear reaction, elements change into other elements called **radioactive elements**. Uranium is a radioactive element. The element uranium breaks down and changes into the element lead. Most natural radioactive elements break down slowly, so energy is released over a long period of time.

**Radioactive particles** are used in the treatment of cancer because they can kill cancer cells. However, if they are powerful enough, they can also cause death. People working around such substances must protect themselves with the correct clothing, equipment, and procedures.

## Sample Test

*DIRECTIONS: Read each item and select the best response.*

1. **Which of the following data sets is properly represented by a bar graph?**
   *(Average Rigor) (Skill 1.1)*

   A. Number of people choosing to buy cars, vs. Color of car bought
   B. Number of people choosing to buy cars, vs. Age of car customer
   C. Number of people choosing to buy cars, vs. Distance from car lot to customer home
   D. Number of people choosing to buy cars, vs. Time since last car purchase

2. **A scientist exposes mice to cigarette smoke and notes that their lungs develop tumors. Mice that were not exposed to the smoke do not develop as many tumors. Which of the following conclusions may be drawn from these results?**

   I. Cigarette smoke causes lung tumors.
   II. Cigarette smoke exposure has a positive correlation with lung tumors in mice.
   III. Some mice are predisposed to develop lung tumors.
   IV. Cigarette smoke exposure has a positive correlation with lung tumors in humans.

   *(Rigorous) (Skill 1.1)*

   A. I and II only
   B. II only
   C. I, II, III and IV
   D. II and IV only

3. **Which is the correct order of methodology?**

1. Collecting data
2. Planning a controlled experiment
3. Drawing a conclusion
4. Hypothesizing a result
5. Revisiting a hypothesis to answer a question
*(Easy) (Skill 1.2)*

A. 1,2,3,4,5
B. 4,2,1,3,5
C. 4,5,1,3,2
D. 1,3,4,5,2

4. **For her first project of the year, a student is designing a science experiment to test the effects of light and water on plant growth. You should recommend that she**

_____.

*(Average Rigor) (Skill 1.3)*

A. manipulate the temperature also
B. manipulate the water pH also
C. determine the relationship between light and water unrelated to plant growth
D. omit either water or light as a variable

5. **In an experiment measuring the inhibition effect of different antibiotic discs on bacteria grown in Petri dishes, what are the independent and dependent variables respectively?** *(Rigorous) (Skill 1.3)*

A. number of bacterial colonies and the antibiotic type
B. antibiotic type and the distance between antibiotic and the closest colony
C. antibiotic type and the number of bacterial colonies
D. presence of bacterial colonies and the antibiotic type

6. **Under a 440x power microscope, an object with diameter 0.1 millimeter appears to have a diameter of _____ .** *(Easy) (Skill 1.4)*

A. 4.4 millimeters
B. 44 millimeters
C. 440 millimeters
D. 4400 millimeters

7. **Experiments may be done with any of the following animals except _____ .** *(Rigorous) (Skill 1.5)*

A. birds
B. invertebrates
C. lower order life
D. frogs

8. When measuring the volume of water in a graduated cylinder, where does one read the measurement?
*(Average Rigor) (Skill 1.6)*

A. at the highest point of the liquid
B. at the bottom of the meniscus curve
C. at the closest mark to the top of the liquid
D. at the top of the plastic safety ring

9. In a science experiment, a student needs to repeatly dispense very small measured amounts of liquid into a well-mixed solution. Which of the following is the best choice for his/her equipment to use?
*(Rigorous) (Skill 1.6)*

A. Pipette, Stirring Rod, Beaker
B. Burette with Burette Stand, Stir-plate, Beaker
C. Volumetric Flask, Dropper, Stirring Rod
D. Beaker, Graduated Cylinder, Stir-plate

10. Many times science teachers are faced with the dilemma of not having enough funds to perform all the wonderful science laboratory exercises that they find. Which of these items might help with this problem? *(Easy) (Skill 1.7)*

A. getting supplies at hardware and grocery stores
B. applying for grant money
C. use of school gardens or natural areas.
D. All of the above

11. In which situation would a science teacher be legally liable?
*(Average Rigor) (Skill 1.8)*

A. The teacher leaves the classroom for a telephone call and a student slips and injures him/herself.
B. A student removes his/her goggles and gets acid in his/her eye.
C. A faulty gas line in the classroom causes a fire.
D. A student cuts him/herself with a dissection scalpel.

12. Accepted procedures for preparing solutions should be made with _____ .
*(Average Rigor) (Skill 1.9)*

A. alcohol
B. hydrochloric acid
C. distilled water
D. tap water

13. **Separating blood into blood cells and plasma involves the process of _____ .**
    *(Average Rigor) (Skill 1.10)*

    A. electrophoresis
    B. centrifugation
    C. spectrophotometry
    D. chromatography

14. **Electrophoresis uses electrical charges of molecules to separate them according to their _____ .**
    *(Rigorous) (Skill 1.10)*

    A. polarization
    B. size
    C. type
    D. Shape

15. **What is specific gravity?**
    *(Average Rigor) (Skill 2.1)*

    A. the mass of an object
    B. the ratio of the density of a substance to the density of water
    C. the density of an object
    D. the pull of Earth's gravity on an object

16. **A seltzer tablet changing into bubbles is an example of _____.**
    *(Rigorous) (Skill 2.1)*

    A. a physical change
    B. a chemical change
    C. conversion
    D. diffusion

17. **When heat is added to most solids, they expand. Why is this the case?**
    *(Average Rigor) (Skill 2.2)*

    A. The molecules get bigger.
    B. The faster molecular motion leads to greater distance between the molecules.
    C. The molecules develop greater repelling electric forces.
    D. The molecules form a more rigid structure.

18. **The relationships between pressure and temperature and between temperature and volume are examples of _____.**
    *(Average Rigor) (Skill 2.3)*

    A. indirect variations
    B. direct variations
    C. Boyle's Law
    D. Charles' Law

19. **If the volume of a confined gas is increased, what happens to the pressure of the gas? You may assume that the gas behaves ideally, and that temperature and number of gas molecules remain constant.**
    *(Rigorous) (Skill 2.3)*

    A. The pressure increases.
    B. The pressure decreases.
    C. The pressure stays the same.
    D. There is not enough information given to answer this question.

20. **Vinegar is an example of a _____.**

    *(Easy) (Skill 2.4)*

    A. strong acid
    B. strong base
    C. weak acid
    D. weak base

21. **The Law of Conservation of Energy states that _____.**

    *(Easy) (Skill 2.5)*

    A. There must be the same number of products and reactants in any chemical equation.
    B. Objects always fall toward large masses such as planets.
    C. Energy is neither created nor destroyed, but may change form.
    D. Lights must be turned off when not in use, by state regulation.

22. **Which of the following is a correct definition for "chemical equilibrium"?**

    A. Chemical equilibrium is when the forward and backward reaction rates are equal. The reaction may continue to proceed forward and backward.
    B. Chemical equilibrium is when the forward and backward reaction rates are equal, and equal to zero. The reaction does not continue.
    C. Chemical equilibrium is when there are equal quantities of reactants and products.
    D. Chemical equilibrium is when acids and bases neutralize each other fully.

23. **Based on the description of the model of atom below, give the name of the individual(s) who developed the model.**

    1. **Matter is made up of atoms.**
    2. **Atoms of an element are similar to each other.**
    3. **Atoms of different elements are different from each other.**
    4. **Atoms combine with each other to form new kinds of compounds.**
    *(Rigorous) (Skill 2.6)*

    A. Ernest Rutherford
    B. Neils Bohr
    C. John Dalton
    D. Democritus Thompson

24. **What part of an atom has to change to create another isotope of an element?** *(Rigorous) (Skill 2.7)*

   A. the number of electrons
   B. the number of neutrons
   C. the arrangement of the electrons
   D. the number of protons

25. **The elements in the modern Periodic Table are arranged _____ .**

   *(Easy) (Skill 2.8)*

   A. in numerical order by atomic number
   B. randomly
   C. in alphabetical order by chemical symbol
   D. in numerical order by atomic mass

26. **Which group of metals is the most chemical active?** *(Average Rigor) (Skill 2.8)*

   A. Alkaline earth metals
   B. Transition elements
   C. Alkali metals
   D. Metalloids

27. **Which of the following is not a property of metalloids?** *(Rigorous) (Skill 2.9)*

   A. Metalloids are solids at standard temperature and pressure.
   B. Metalloids can conduct electricity to a limited extent.
   C. Metalloids are found in groups 13 through 17.
   D. Metalloids all favor ionic bonding.

28. **The electrons in an atom used to form a chemical bond are called _____.** *(Average Rigor) (Skill 2.10)*

   A. outer shell electrons
   B. excited electrons
   C. valence electrons
   D. reactive electrons

29. **Carbon bonds with hydrogen by _____ .** *(Rigorous) (Skill 2.10)*

   A. ionic bonding
   B. non-polar covalent bonding
   C. polar covalent bonding
   D. strong nuclear force

30. **Which reaction below is a decomposition reaction?**
*(Rigorous) (Skill 2.11)*

   A. $HCl + NaOH \rightarrow NaCl + H_2O$
   B. $C + O_2 \rightarrow CO_2$
   C. $2H_2O \rightarrow 2H_2 + O_2$
   D. $CuSO_4 + Fe \rightarrow FeSO_4 + Cu$

31. **The theory of "sea floor spreading" explains _____.**
*(Average Rigor) (Skill 3.1)*

   A. the shapes of the continents
   B. how continents collide
   C. how continents move apart
   D. how continents sink to become part of the ocean floor

32. **_____ are cracks in the plates of the earth's crust, along which the plates move.**
*(Easy) (Skill 3.2)*

   A. Faults
   B. Ridges
   C. Earthquakes
   D. Volcanoes

33. **Although Yellowstone has many unique geological features, its entirety is encompassed by one type of geological feature. What is that feature?**
*(Rigorous) (Skill 3.2)*

   A. Caldera
   B. Glacial trough
   C. Shield volcano
   D. Laccolith

34. **Fossils of a dinosaur genus known as *Saurolophus* have been found in both western North America and in Mongolia. What is the most likely explanation for these findings?**
*(Rigorous) (Skill 3.3)*

   A. Convergent evolution
   B. This genus of dinosaurs was powerful swimmers that swam across the Bering Strait.
   C. At one time, all land masses were connected in a landform known as Pangaea, so, the dinosaurs could have easily walked from what is now Mongolia to what is now western North America.
   D. Although Asia and North America were separate continents at the time, low sea levels made it possible for the dinosaurs to walk from one continent to the other.

35. The end of a geologic era is most often characterized by
_____.
*(Average Rigor) (Skill 3.4)*

A. a general uplifting of the crust
B. the extinction of the dominant plants and animals
C. the appearance of new life forms
D. All of the above

36. Which of the following is the best explanation of the fundamental concept of uniformitarianism?
*(Rigorous) (Skill 3.4)*

A. The types and varieties of life between will see a uniform progression over time.
B. The physical, chemical and biological laws that operate in the geologic past operate in the same way today.
C. Debris from catastrophic events (i.e., volcanoes and meteorites) will be evenly distributed over the affected area.
D. The frequency and intensity of major geologic events will remain consistent over long periods of time.

37. A contour line that has tiny comb-like lines along the inner edge indicates
a_____.
*(Average Rigor) (Skill 3.5)*

A. depression
B. mountain
C. valley
D. river

38. Surface ocean currents are caused by which of the following?
*(Average Rigor) (Skill 3.6)*

A. Earth's rotation
B. Density changes in water
C. Wind
D. Tidal forces

39. Neap tides are especially weak tides that occur when the Sun and Moon are in a perpindicular arrangment to Earth, and spring tides are espically strong tides that occur when the Sun and Moon are in line. At which combination of lunar phases do these tides occur (respectively)?
*(Rigorous) (Skill 3.6)*

A. Half Moon and full Moon
B. Quarter Moon and New Moon
C. Gibbous Moon and Quarter Moon
D. Full Moon and New Moon

40. **Which of these best decribes the seafloor along the majority of the Pacific shoreline?**
*(Average Rigor) (Skill 3.7)*

A. Continental slope
B. Continental rise
C. Continental shelf
D. Seamount

41. **Mount Kīlauea on the island of Hawaii is a very active volcano that has continuous lava flow into the ocean near it. What is the name of the type of shoreline created at the point where the lava flows meet the water?**
*(Rigorous) (Skill 3.7)*

A. Stacking
B. Submerged
C. Developing
D. Emergent

42. **The salinity of ocean water is closest to _____.**
*(Average Rigor) (Skill 3.8)*

A. 0.035 %
B. 0.35 %
C. 3.5 %
D. 35 %

43. **Igneous rocks can be classified according to which of the following?**
*(Easy) (Skill 3.9)*

A. Texture
B. Composition
C. Formation process.
D. All of the above

44. **Lithification refers to one process to create**

_____.
*(Rigorous) (Skill 3.9)*

A. metamorphic rocks
B. sedimentary rocks
C. igneous rocks
D. lithium oxide

45. **Which of these is a true statement about loamy soil?**
*(Average Rigor) (Skill 3.10)*

A. Loamy soil is gritty and porous.
B. Loamy soil is smooth and a good barrier to water.
C. Loamy soil is hostile to microorganisms.
D. Loamy soil is velvety and clumpy.

46. **Which of the following is the most accurate definition of a nonrenewable resource?** *(Average Rigor) (Skill 3.11)*

A. A nonrenewable resource is never replaced once used.
B. A nonrenewable resource is replaced on a timescale that is very long relative to human life-spans.
C. A nonrenewable resource is a resource that can only be manufactured by humans.
D. A nonrenewable resource is a species that has already become extinct.

47. **Recently, New Hampshire's famous "Old Man in the Mountain" collapsed. What type of erosion was the principal cause of this?** *(Rigorous) (Skill 3.12)*

A. Physical weathering
B. Chemical weathering
C. Exfoliation
D. Frost wedging

48. **A telescope that collects light by using a concave mirror and can produce small images is called a _____.** *(Easy) (Skill 3.13)*

A. radio telescope
B. reflecting telescope
C. refracting telescope
D. orbital telescope

49. **A star's brightness is referred to as _____.** *(Average Rigor) (Skill 3.13)*

A. magnitude
B. mass
C. apparent magnitude
D. intensity

50. **Which of the following is the best definition for "meteorite"?** *(Easy) (Skill 3.14)*

A. A meteorite is a mineral composed of mica and feldspar.
B. A meteorite is material from outer space that has struck the earth's surface.
C. A meteorite is an element that has properties of both metals and nonmetals.
D. A meteorite is a very small unit of length measurement.

51. **The planet with true retrograde rotation is _____.** *(Rigorous) (Skill 3.14)*

A. Pluto
B. Uranus
C. Venus
D. Saturn

52. **Earth's galaxy is found in the Milky Way. What kind of galaxy is it?**
*(Average Rigor) (Skill 3.15)*

A. Irregular
B. Elliptical
C. Conical
D. Spiral

53. **What is the main difference between the "condensation hypothesis" and the "tidal hypothesis" for the origin of the solar system?**
*(Rigorous) (Skill 3.16)*

A. The tidal hypothesis can be tested, but the condensation hypothesis cannot.
B. The tidal hypothesis proposes a near collision of two stars pulling on each other, but the condensation hypothesis proposes condensation of rotating clouds of dust and gas.
C. The tidal hypothesis explains how tides began on planets such as Earth, but the condensation hypothesis explains how water vapor became liquid on Earth.
D. The tidal hypothesis is based on Aristotelian physics, but the condensation hypothesis is based on Newtonian mechanics.

54. **What are the most significant and prevalent elements in the biosphere?**
*(Easy) (Skill 3.17)*

A. Carbon, hydrogen, oxygen, nitrogen, phosphorus
B. Carbon, hydrogen, sodium, iron, calcium
C. Carbon, oxygen, sulfur, manganese, iron
D. Carbon, hydrogen, oxygen, nickel, sodium, nitrogen

55. **What makes up the largest abiotic portion of the nitrogen cycle?**
*(Average Rigor) (Skill 3.17)*

A. Nitrogen fixing bacteria
B. Nitrates
C. Decomposers
D. Atmosphere

56. **Which type of cloud is most likely to produce precipitation?**
*(Average Rigor) (Skill 3.18)*

A. Cirrocumulus
B. Stratocumulus
C. Cumulonimbus
D. Cirrostratus

57. Air moving northward from the horse latitudes produces a belt of winds called the _____.
(Rigorous) (Skill 3.18)

A. Prevailing Westerlies
B. North westerlies
C. trade winds
D. Prevailing Easterlies

58. Moss and lichen are found within polar ice in which climate?
(Average Rigor) (Skill 3.19)

A. Taiga
B. Grasslands
C. Tundra
D. Rainforests

59. Which is a form of precipitation?
(Rigorous) (Skill 3.20)

A. Snow
B. Frost
C. Fog
D. All of the above

60. When water falls to a cave floor and evaporates, it may deposit calcium carbonate. This process leads to the formation of which of the following?
(Easy) (Skill 3.21)

A. Stalactites
B. Stalagmites
C. Fault lines
D. Sedimentary rocks

61. Quicksand is created by the interaction of very fine sand and water. The process that creates quicksand is called
_____ .
(Rigorous) (Skill 3.21)

A. absorption
B. percolation
C. leaching
D. runoff

62. What is the source for most of the United States' drinking water?
(Rigorous) (Skill 3.22)

A. Desalinated ocean water
B. Surface water (lakes, streams, mountain runoff)
C. Rainfall into municipal reservoirs
D. Groundwater

63. Contamination may enter groundwater by _____.
(Easy) (Skill 3.23)

A. air pollution
B. leaking septic tanks
C. photochemical processes
D. sewage treatment plants

64. **Which of the following is not a common type of acid in "acid rain" or acidified surface water?**
*(Average Rigor) (Skill 3.24)*

A. Nitric acid
B. Sulfuric acid
C. Carbonic acid
D. Hydrofluoric acid

65. **Identify the correct sequence of organization of living things from lower to higher order.**
*(Average Rigor) (Skill 4.1)*

A. Cell, organelle, organ, tissue, system, organism
B. Cell, tissue, organ, organelle, system, organism
C. Organelle, cell, tissue, organ, system, organism
D. Organelle, tissue, cell, organ, system, organism

66. **Which of the following is not a necessary characteristic of living things?**
*(Average Rigor) (Skill 4.2)*

A. Movement
B. Reduction of local entropy
C. Ability to cause change in local energy form
D. Reproduction

67. **Which of the following is not one of the principles of Darwin's idea of natural selection?**
*(Average Rigor) (Skill 4.3)*

A. More individuals are produced than will survive.
B. The individuals in a certain species vary from generation to generation.
C. Only the fittest members of a species survive.
D. Some genes allow for better survival of an animal.

68. **What is the principle driving force for evolution of antibiotic resistant bacteria?**
*(Rigorous) (Skill 4.3)*

A. Mutation
B. Reproduction method
C. Population size
D. Emigration

69. **What cell organelle contains the cell's stored food?**
*(Rigorous) (Skill 4.4)*

A. Vacuoles
B. Golgi apparatus
C. Ribosomes
D. Lysosomes

70. **The first stage of mitosis is called _____ .**
*(Average Rigor) (Skill 4.5)*

A. telophase
B. anaphase
C. prophase
D. mitophase

71. **Which process results in a haploid chromosome number?**
(Rigorous) (Skill 4.5)

   A. Mitosis
   B. Meiosis I
   C. Meiosis II
   D. Neither mitosis nor meiosis

72. **Klinefelter Syndrome is a condition in which a person is born with two X chromosomes and one Y chromosome. What process during meiosis would cause this to happen?**
(Rigorous) (Skill 4.6)

   A. Inversion
   B. Translocation
   C. Nondisjunction
   D. Arrangement failure

73. **Animal cells differ from plant cells because they have _____.**
(Average Rigor) (Skill 4.7)

   A. vacuoles
   B. hair cells
   C. epidermal cells
   D. centrioles

74. **In the Law of Dominance _____**
(Easy) (Skill 4.8)

   A. only one of the two possible alleles from each parent is passed on to the offspring.
   B. alleles sort independently of each other.
   C. one trait may cover up the allele of the other trait.
   D. flowers have white alleles and purple alleles.

75. **A white flower is crossed with a red flower. Which of the following is a sign of incomplete dominance?**
(Average Rigor) (Skill 4.8)

   A. Pink flowers
   B. Red flowers
   C. White flowers
   D. No flowers

76. **A carrier of a genetic disorder is heterozygous for a disorder that is recessive in nature. Hemophilia is a sex-linked disorder. What does this mean?**
(Easy) (Skill 4.9)

   A. Only females can be carriers.
   B. Only males can be carriers.
   C. Both males and females can be carriers.
   D. Neither females nor males can be carriers.

77. An Arabic horse's purebred bloodline makes it a good example of _____.
(Rigorous) (Skill 4.9)

A. a homozygous animal
B. a heterozygous animal
C. codominance
D. a polygenic character

78. Which of the following is not a nucleotide?
(Average Rigor) (Skill 4.10)

A. Adenine
B. Alanine
C. Cytosine
D. Guanine

79. Amino acids are carried to the ribosome in protein synthesis by _____ .
(Rigorous) (Skill 4.10)

A. transfer RNA (tRNA)
B. transport enzymes
C. ribosomal RNA (rNA)
D. cytoskeletal transport proteins

80. Which of the following features is/are found in eukaryotic cells but not in prokaryotic cells?

1. Nucleus
2. Mitochondria
3. Cytoskeleton
4. Vacules
(Easy) (Skill 4.11)

A. 4 Only
B. 1 and 2
C. 1, 2 and 4
D. 1, 2 and 3

81. Which of the following is not a member of Kingdom Fungi?
(Easy) (Skill 4.12)

A. Mold
B. Blue-green algae
C. Mildew
D. Mushrooms

82. Diatoms are one of the primary contributors to photosynthesis in the oceans. They also have a unique cell wall made up of silicate, which often makes them sink in the water. Although some diatoms might form colonies, most are single celled. Diatoms are usually nonmotile, although in many species the gametes have flagella. Based on this information, which answer is the best identification of diatoms? *(Rigorous) (Skill 4.12)*

A. Protozoans
B. Euglenas
C. Protists
D. Blue-Green Algae

83. Extensive use of antibacterial soap has been found to increase the virulence of certain infections in hospitals. Which of the following might be an explanation for this phenomenon? *(Average Rigor) (Skill 4.13)*

A. Antibacterial soaps do not kill viruses.
B. Antibacterial soaps do not incorporate the same antibiotics used as medicine.
C. Antibacterial soaps kill a lot of bacteria, and only the hardiest ones survive to reproduce.
D. Antibacterial soaps can be very drying to the skin.

84. Which part of a plant is responsible for transporting water. *(Easy) (Skill 4.14)*

A. Phloem
B. Xylem
C. Stomata
D. Cortex

85. Which plant tissues contain chloroplasts? *(Average Rigor) (Skill 4.14)*

A. Stomata
B. Palisade mesophyll
C. Spongy Mesophyll
D. Endosperm

86. As in all processess, plant growth must deal with the Law of Conservation of Mass and Energy. Most people recongize the sun as the source of a plant's energy. What is the primary source of the introduction of mass? *(Rigorous) (Skill 4.15)*

A. Water absorbed through the roots.
B. Nutrient's and minerals absorbed through the roots.
C. Carbon absorbed through the roots.
D. Carbon absorbed through the stomata.

87. **Which of the following organisms use spores to reproduce?**
*(Average Rigor) (Skill 4.16)*

   A. Fish
   B. Flowering plants
   C. Conifers
   D. Ferns

88. **Which of the following is not characteristic of Gymnosperms?**
*(Rigorous) (Skill 4.16)*

   A. They are less dependent on water to assist in reproduction than other plant groups.
   B. Gymnosperms have cones that protect their seeds.
   C. Gymnosperms reproduce asexually.
   D. Gymnosperm seeds and pollen are easily carried by the wind.

89. **Mollusca have an open circulatory system. Their sinuses serve which purposes?**
*(Rigorous) (Skill 4.17)*

   A. Breathing
   B. Bathing
   C. Filtering food
   D. Circulating blood

90. **Which is the correct sequence of insect development?**
*(Easy) (Skill 4.18)*

   A. Egg, pupa, larva, adult
   B. Egg, larva, pupa, adult
   C. Egg, adult, larva, pupa
   D. Pupa, egg, larva, adult

91. **The two strands of a DNA molecule are held together by what kind of bond?**
*(Average Rigor) (Skill 4.18)*

   A. Polar-covalent
   B. Ionic
   C. Non-polar covalent
   D. Hydrogen

92. **Many male birds sing long, complicated songs that describe thier identity and the area of land that they claim. Which of the answers below is the best decription of this behavior?**
*(Rigorous) (Skill 4.19)*

   A. Innate territorial behavior
   B. Learned competitive behavior
   C. Innate mating behavior
   D. Learned territorial behavior

93. **Echinodermata are best known for which characteristic?**
*(Average Rigor) (Skill 4.20)*

   A. Their slimy skin
   B. Their dry habitat
   C. Their tube feet
   D. Their tentacles

94. **Which of the following animals are most likely to live in a tropical rainforest?** *(Easy) (Skill 4.21)*

    A. Reindeer
    B. Monkeys
    C. Puffins
    D. Bears

95. **Which one of the following biomes makes up the greatest percentage of the biosphere?** *(Rigorous) (Skill 4.21)*

    A. Desert
    B. Tropical rainforest
    C. Marine
    D. Temperate deciduous forest

96. **Which of the following terms does not describe a way that the human race has had a negative impact on the biosphere?** *(Rigorous) (Skill 4.22)*

    A. Biological magnification
    B. Pollution
    C. Carrying capacity
    D. Simplification of the food web

97. **Multiple Sclerosis is an autoimmune disease that prevents nerves that are being attacked from being properly insulated, thus preventing normal propagation of the nerve signal. Which part of the nervous system is the most likely target of the body's immune system in this diease?** *(Rigorous) (Skill 4.23)*

    A. Axon
    B. Synapse
    C. Dendrite
    D. Myelin

98. **Which of the following is not a way in which alcohol, drugs, or tobacco affect the normal processes of the human body?** *(Average Rigor) (Skill 4.24)*

    A. Absorption of nutrients
    B. Interference with physical and mental development
    C. Damaging developing organs
    D. Boosting the immune system

99. **Water inside a closed vessel is in thermal equilibrium in all three states (ice, water, and vapor) at 273.15 degrees in what measurement scale?** *(Average Rigor) (Skill 5.1)*

    A. Fahrenheit
    B. Celsius
    C. BTU (British Thermal Unit)
    D. Kelvin

100. The transfer of heat by electromagnetic waves is called _____
(Easy) (Skill 5.2)

   A. conduction
   B. convection
   C. phase change
   D. radiation

101. When you step out of the shower, the floor feels colder on your feet than the bathmat. Which of the following is the correct explanation for this phenomenon?
(Rigorous) (Skill 5.2)

   A. The floor is colder than the bathmat.
   B. The bathmat being smaller that the floor quickly reaches equilibrium with your body temperature.
   C. Heat is conducted more easily into the floor.
   D. Water is absorbed from your feet into the bathmat so it doesn't evaporate as quickly as it does off the floor thus not cooling the bathmat as quickly.

102. Energy is measured with the same units as _____.
(Average Rigor) (Skill 5.3)

   A. force
   B. momentum
   C. work
   D. power

103. A boulder sitting on the edge of a cliff has which type of energy?
(Easy) (Skill 5.4)

   A. Kinetic energy
   B. Latent Energy
   C. No energy
   D. Potential energy

104. Newton's Laws are taught in science classes because _____
(Rigorous) (Skill 5.4)

   A. they are the correct analysis of inertia, gravity, and forces.
   B. they are a close approximation to correct physics, for usual Earth conditions.
   C. they accurately incorporate relativity into studies of forces.
   D. Newton was a well-respected scientist in his time.

105. **Which of the following is a correct explanation for an astronaut's "weightlessness"?**
*(Average Rigor) (Skill 5.5)*

A. Astronauts continue to feel the pull of gravity in space, but they are so far from planets that the force is small.
B. Astronauts continue to feel the pull of gravity in space, but spacecraft have such powerful engines that those forces dominate, reducing effective weight.
C. Astronauts do not feel the pull of gravity in space because space is a vacuum.
D. The cumulative gravitational forces that the astronaut is experiencing from all sources in the solar system equal to a net gravitational force of zero.

107. **The picture shows a view from slightly above a teacher swinging a yo-yo over their head. The teacher would be holding onto the string in the center of the circle, and the circle itself describes the path of the yoyo. Arrows 1,2 and 3 describe the forces on the yoyo. Which answer below names the forces correctly?**
*(Rigorous) (Skill 5.5)*

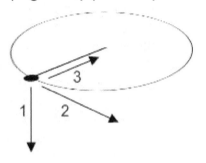

A. 1 is inertia, 2 is centripetal force, 3 is gravity
B. 1 is centripetal force, 2 is gravity, 3 is inertia
C. 1 is gravity, 2 is inertia, 3 is centripetal
D. 1 is gravity, 2 is inertia, 3 is centrifugal

107. **A grooved wheel turned by a cord or a chain is what kind of simple machine?**
*(Easy) (Skill 5.6)*

A. Lever
B. Inclined Plane
C. Pulley
D. Wheel and Axle

108. Work done divided by the amount of time to do it is called its _____.
*(Easy) (Skill 5.7)*

A. energy
B. heat
C. power
D. efficiency

109. You have four pulley setups (in order to solve the problem you don't need the number and size of the pulleys), each with a weight of 1 Newton attched at one end. Based on the energy used to lift the mass and how far the mass was lifted, which of the systems was the most efficient?
*(Rigorous) (Skill 5.7)*

A. 3 Joules lifted the mass 2 meters
B. 10 Joules lifted the mass 8 meters
C. 4 Joules lifted the mass 3.6 meters
D. 7.5 Joules lifted the mass 6 meters

110. Sound can be transmitted in all of the following except _____.
*(Easy) (Skill 5.8)*

A. air
B. water
C. a diamond
D. a vacuum

111. Sonar works by _____.
*(Easy) (Skill 5.10)*

A. timing how long it takes sound to reach a certain speed
B. bouncing sound waves between two metal plates
C. bouncing sound waves off an underwater object and timing how long it takes for the sound to return
D. evaluating the motion and amplitude of sound

112. As a train approaches, the whistle sounds get _____
*(Rigorous) (Skill 5.10)*

A. higher, because it has a higher apparent frequency.
B. lower, because it has a lower apparent frequency
C. higher, because it has a lower apparent frequency.
D. lower, because it has a higher apparent frequency

113. The speed of light is different in different materials. This is responsible for _____.
*(Average Rigor) (Skill 5.11)*

A. interference
B. refraction
C. reflection
D. relativity

114. Cameras use what kind of lens to produce an image on film?
*(Average Rigor) (Skill 5.12)*

A. Concave
B. Convex
C. Convergent
D. Polarized

115. When does a converging lens produce a real image?
*(Rigorous) (Skill 5.12)*

A. Always
B. Never
C. When the object is within one focal length of the lens.
D. When the object is further than one focal length from the lens.

116. Which of the following is not a characteristic of all electrically charged objects?
*(Average Rigor) (Skill 5.14)*

A. Opposites attract
B. Like repels like
C. Charge is conserved
D. A magnetic charge develops

117. In Ohm's Law (I=V/R), what does the V represents?
*(Average Rigor) (Skill 5.15)*

A. Current
B. Amperes
C. Potential Difference
D. Resistance

118. A 10 ohm resistor and a 50 ohm resistor are connected in parallel. If the current in the 10 ohm resistor is 5 amperes, the current (in amperes) running through the 50 ohm resistor is ____.
*(Average Rigor) (Skill 5.16)*

A. 1
B. 50
C. 250
D. 6

119. A light bulb is connected in series with a rotating coil within a magnetic field. The brightness of the light may be increased by any of the following except _____.
*(Rigorous) (Skill 5.16)*

A. rotating the coil more rapidly.
B. using more loops in the coil.
C. using a different color wire for the coil.
D. using a stronger magnetic field.

120. Which component(s) of an atom is most responsible for the development of a magnetic field in an object?
*(Average Rigor) (Skill 5.17)*

A. Electrons
B. Protons
C. Neutrons
D. Electrons and protons

121. **Identify which of the answers has correctly paired the terms with their definitions?**

I. Amperes  1. Electrical potential
II. Volts      2. Electrical resistance
III. Ohms    3. Energy flow
IV. Watts   4. Electric current

*(Rigorous) (Skill 5.17)*

    A. I:1, II:3, III:4, IV:2
    B. I:3, II:1, III:2, IV:4
    C. I:4, II:1, III:2, IV:3
    D. I:3, II:4, III:2, IV:3

122. **Which of the following is not a way to make an electromagnet more powerful?**
*(Rigorous) (Skill 5.17)*

    A. Make more coils
    B. Put an iron core (nail) inside the coil
    C. Use more battery power
    d. Make the coils tighter

123. **Hoover Dam is perhaps the most famous hydro-electric dam in North America. Which one of the follwing best describes how hydroelectric dams generate their power?**
*(Rigorous) (Skill 5.18)*

    A. Gravity imparts kinetic energy onto the falling water, which acts as a mechanical force turning the generator turbines. The turbines contain a coil of wire, and as the turbine spins it spins the coil of wire. This generates an electrical current in the wire that is then sent out to the power grid.

    B. Gravity imparts kinetic energy onto the falling water, which acts as a mechanical force turning the generator turbines. When the turbines spin, they spin a series of electromagnets inside a coil of copper wire. This generates an electrical current in the wire that is then sent out to the power grid.

    C. Gravity imparts potential energy onto the falling water, which acts as a mechanical force turning the generator turbines. When the turbines spin, they spin a series of electromagnets inside a coil of copper wire. This generates an electrical current in the wire that is then sent out to the power grid.

    D. Gravity imparts kinetic energy onto the falling water, which acts as a mechanical force turning the generator turbines. When the turbines spin, they spin a series of permanent magnets inside a coil of copper wire. This generates an electrical current in the wire that is then sent out to the power grid.

124. **What is the main obstacle to using nuclear fusion for obtaining electricity?**
*(Average Rigor) (Skill 5.19)*

    A. Nuclear fusion produces much more pollution than nuclear fission.

    B. There is no obstacle; most power plants use nuclear fusion today.

    C. Nuclear fusion requires very high temperature and activation energy.

    D. The fuel for nuclear fusion is extremely expensive.

125. **In a fission reactor, "heavy water" is used to**

    _____ .

*(Rigorous) (Skill 5.19)*

    A. terminate fission reactions

    B. slow down neutrons and moderate reactions

    C. rehydrate the chemicals

    D. initiate a chain reaction

## Answer Key

| | | | | | | | | | |
|---|---|---|---|---|---|---|---|---|---|
| 1. | a | 26. | c | 51. | c | 76. | a | 101. | c |
| 2. | b | 27. | d | 52. | d | 77. | a | 102. | c |
| 3. | b | 28. | c | 53. | b | 78. | b | 103. | d |
| 4. | d | 29. | c | 54. | a | 79. | a | 104. | b |
| 5. | b | 30. | c | 55. | d | 80. | d | 105. | a |
| 6. | b | 31. | c | 56. | c | 81. | b | 106. | c |
| 7. | a | 32. | a | 57. | a | 82. | c | 107. | c |
| 8. | b | 33. | a | 58. | c | 83. | c | 108. | c |
| 9. | b | 34. | d | 59. | a | 84. | b | 109. | c |
| 10. | d | 35. | d | 60. | b | 85. | b | 110. | d |
| 11. | a | 36. | b | 61. | b | 86. | d | 111. | c |
| 12. | c | 37. | a | 62. | d | 87. | d | 112. | a |
| 13. | b | 38. | c | 63. | b | 88. | c | 113. | b |
| 14. | b | 39. | b | 64. | d | 89. | b | 114. | b |
| 15. | b | 40. | c | 65. | c | 90. | b | 115. | d |
| 16. | b | 41. | d | 66. | a | 91. | d | 116. | d |
| 17. | b | 42. | c | 67. | c | 92. | d | 117. | c |
| 18. | b | 43. | d | 68. | c | 93. | c | 118. | a |
| 19. | b | 44. | b | 69. | a | 94. | b | 119. | c |
| 20. | c | 45. | d | 70. | c | 95. | c | 120. | a |
| 21. | c | 46. | b | 71. | c | 96. | c | 121. | c |
| 22. | a | 47. | d | 72. | c | 97. | d | 122. | d |
| 23. | c | 48. | b | 73. | d | 98. | d | 123. | b |
| 24. | b | 49. | a | 74. | c | 99. | d | 124. | c |
| 25. | a | 50. | b | 75. | a | 100. | d | 125. | b |

## Rigor Table

|  | Easy<br>%20 | Average Rigor<br>%40 | Rigorous<br>%40 |
|---|---|---|---|
| Question # | 3, 6, 10, 20, 21, 25, 32, 43, 48, 50, 54, 60, 63, 74, 76, 80, 81, 84, 90, 94, 100, 103, 107, 108, 110, 111 | 1, 4, 8, 11, 12, 13, 15, 17, 18, 22, 26, 28, 31, 35, 37, 38, 40, 42, 45, 46, 49, 52, 55, 56, 58, 64, 65, 66, 67, 70, 73, 75, 78, 83, 85, 87, 91, 93, 98, 99, 102, 105, 113, 114, 116, 117, 118, 120, 124 | 2, 5, 7, 9, 14, 16, 19, 23, 24, 27, 29, 30, 33, 34, 36, 39, 41, 44, 47, 51, 53, 57, 59, 61, 62, 68, 69, 71, 72, 77, 79, 82, 86, 88, 89, 92, 95, 96, 97, 101, 104, 106, 109, 112, 115, 119, 121, 122, 123, 125 |

## Rationales with Sample Questions

1. **Which of the following data sets is properly represented by a bar graph?**
   *(Average Rigor) (Skill 1.1)*

a. Number of people choosing to buy cars, vs. Color of car bought
b. Number of people choosing to buy cars, vs. Age of car customer
c. Number of people choosing to buy cars, vs. Distance from car lot to customer home
d. Number of people choosing to buy cars, vs. Time since last car purchase

**Answer: a. Number of people choosing to buy cars, vs. Color of car bought.**

A bar graph should be used only for data sets in which the independent variable is non-continuous (discrete), e.g. gender, color, etc. Any continuous independent variable (age, distance, time, etc.) should yield a scatter-plot when the dependent variable is plotted. Therefore, the answer must be (a).

2. A scientist exposes mice to cigarette smoke, and notes that their lungs develop tumors. Mice that were not exposed to the smoke do not develop as many tumors. Which of the following conclusions may be drawn from these results?:

I. Cigarette smoke causes lung tumors.
II. Cigarette smoke exposure has a positive correlation with lung tumors in mice.
III. Some mice are predisposed to develop lung tumors.
IV. Cigarette smoke exposure has a positive correlation with lung tumors in humans.
*(Rigorous) (Skill 1.1)*

a. I and II only
b. II only
c. I , II, III and IV
d. II and IV only

**Answer: b. II only**

Although cigarette smoke has been found to cause lung tumors (and many other problems), this particular experiment shows only that there is a positive correlation between smoke exposure and tumor development in these mice. It may be true that some mice are more likely to develop tumors than others, which is why a control group of identical mice should have been used for comparison. Mice are often used to model human reactions, but this is as much due to their low financial and emotional cost as it is due to their being a "good model" for humans, and thus this scientist cannot make the conclusion that cigarette smoke exposure has a positive correlation with lung tumors in humans based on this data alone. Therefore, the answer must be (b).

3.      **Which is the correct order of methodology?**

     1.      **Collecting data**
     2.      **Planning a controlled experiment**
     3.      **Drawing a conclusion**
     4.      **Hypothesizing a result**
     5.      **Revisiting a hypothesis to answer a question**
     *(Easy) (Skill 1.2)*

a.      1,2,3,4,5
b.      4,2,1,3,5
c.      4,5,1,3,2
d.      1,3,4,5,2

**Answer:  b.  4,2,1,3,5**

The correct methodology for the scientific method is first to make a meaningful hypothesis (educated guess), then plan and execute a controlled experiment to test that hypothesis. Using the data collected in that experiment, the scientist then draws conclusions and attempts to answer the original question related to the hypothesis. This is consistent only with answer (b).

4.      **For her first project of the year, a student is designing a science experiment to test the effects of light and water on plant growth. You should recommend that she _____**
     *(Average Rigor) (Skill 1.3)*

a.      manipulate the temperature also.
b.      manipulate the water pH also.
c.      determine the relationship between light and water unrelated to plant growth.
d.      omit either water or light as a variable.

**Answer:  d.  omit either water or light as a variable**

As a science teacher for middle-school-aged kids, it is important to reinforce the idea of 'constant' vs. 'variable' in science experiments. At this level, it is wisest to have only one variable examined in each science experiment. (Later, students can hold different variables constant while investigating others.) Therefore, it is counterproductive to add in other variables (answers (a)or (b)). It is also irrelevant to determine the light-water interactions aside from plant growth (c). So the only possible answer is (d).

5.    In an experiment measuring the inhibition effect of different antibiotic discs on bacteria grown in Petri dishes, what are the independent and dependent variables respectively?
*(Rigorous) (Skill 1.3)*

a.    Number of bacterial colonies and the antibiotic type
b.    Antibiotic type and the distance between antibiotic and the closest colony
c.    Antibiotic type and the number of bacterial colonies
d.    Presence of bacterial colonies and the antibiotic type


**Answer:  b.  Antibiotic type and the distance between antibiotic and the closest colony**

To answer this question, recall that the independent variable in an experiment is the entity that is changed by the scientist, in order to observe the effects the dependent variable. In this experiment, antibiotic used is purposely changed so it is the independent variable. Answers a and d list antibiotic type as the dependent variable and thus cannot be the answer, leaving answers b and c as the only two viable choices. The best answer is b, because it measures at what concentration of the antibiotic the bacteria are able to grow at, (as you move from the source of the antibiotic, the concentration decreases).  Answer c is not as effective because it could be interpreted that a plate that shows a large number of colonies a greater distance from the antibiotic is a less effective antibiotic than a plate a smaller number of colonies in close proximity to the antibiotic disc, which is reverse of the actually result.

6.  **Under a 440x power microscope, an object with diameter 0.1 millimeter appears to have a diameter of _____.**
    *(Easy) (Skill 1.4)*

a.  4.4 millimeters
b.  44 millimeters
c.  440 millimeters
d.  4400 millimeters.

**Answer:  b.  44 millimeters**

To answer this question, recall that to calculate a new length, you multiply the original length by the magnification power of the instrument. Therefore, the 0.1 millimeter diameter is multiplied by 440. This equals 44, so the image appears to be 44 millimeters in diameter. You could also reason that since a 440 power microscope is considered a "high power" microscope, you would expect a 0.1 millimeter object to appear a few centimeters long. Therefore, the correct answer is (b).

7.  **Experiments may be done with any of the following animals except _____ .**
    *(Rigorous) (Skill 1.5)*

a.  birds
b.  invertebrates
c.  lower order life
d.  frogs

**Answer:  a.  birds**

No dissections may be performed on living mammalian vertebrates or birds. Lower order life and invertebrates may be used. Biological experiments may be done with all animals except mammalian vertebrates or birds. Therefore the answer is (a).

8.    **When measuring the volume of water in a graduated cylinder, where does one read the measurement?**
      *(Average Rigor) (Skill 1.6)*

a.    At the highest point of the liquid
b.    At the bottom of the meniscus curve
c.    At the closest mark to the top of the liquid
d.    At the top of the plastic safety ring

**Answer:  b.  At the bottom of the meniscus curve.**

To measure water in glass, you must look at the top surface at eye-level, and ascertain the location of the bottom of the meniscus (the curved surface at the top of the water). The meniscus forms because water molecules adhere to the sides of the glass, which is a slightly stronger force than their cohesion to each other.  This leads to a U-shaped top of the liquid column, the bottom of which gives the most accurate volume measurement. (Other liquids have different forces, e.g. mercury in glass, which has a convex meniscus.) This is consistent only with answer (b).

9.    **In a science experiment, a student needs to repeatedly dispense very small measured amounts of liquid into a well-mixed solution. Which of the following is the best choice for his/her equipment to use?**
      *(Rigorous) (Skill 1.6)*

a.    Pipette, stirring rod, beaker
b.    Burette with burette stand, stir-plate, beaker
c.    Volumetric flask, dropper, stirring rod
d.    Beaker, graduated cylinder, stir-plate

**Answer:  b.  Burette with burette stand, stir-plate, beaker**

The most accurate and convenient way to repeatedly dispense small measured amounts of liquid in the laboratory is with a burette, on a burette stand. To keep a solution well-mixed, a magnetic stir-plate is the most sensible choice, and the solution will usually be mixed in a beaker. Although other combinations of materials could be used for this experiment, choice (b) is thus the simplest and best.  Choices a and c rely on a stirring a rod, which requires the student to try to mix the solution by hand while adding the liquid.  Answer d relies on a graduated cylinder to add the small amounts of liquid to the solution, it is more difficult to add small quantities of a liquid with a graduated cylinder.

10. **Many times science teachers are faced with the dilemma of not having enough funds to perform all the wonderful science laboratory exercises that they find. Which of these items might help with this problem?**
*(Easy) (Skill 1.7)*

a.   Getting supplies at hardware and grocery stores
b.   Applying for grant money
c.   Use of school gardens or natural areas
d.   All of the above

**Answer:  d.  All of the above**

As a teacher, anything you can get to help you teach science, go for it, as long as it doesn't break any laws or put anyone (you or students) in danger. Many common supplies can be found in your local stores. In addition to government grant money, there are many private sources of grant money that you can pursue. Too  often we try to teach about nature while sittng in the classroom, if you can get outdoors, then do so.

11. **In which situation would a science teacher be legally liable?**
*(Average Rigor) (Skill 1.8)*

a.   The teacher leaves the classroom for a telephone call and a student slips and injures him/herself.
b.   A student removes his/her goggles and gets acid in his/her eye.
c.   A faulty gas line in the classroom causes a fire.
d.   A student cuts him/herself with a dissection scalpel.

**Answer:  a.  The teacher leaves the classroom for a telephone call and a student slips and injures him/herself.**

Teachers are required to exercise a "reasonable duty of care" for their students. Accidents may happen (e.g. (d)), or students may make poor decisions (e.g. (B)), or facilities may break down (e.g. (c)). However, the teacher has the responsibility to be present and to do his/her best to create a safe and effective learning environment.  Therefore, the answer is (a).

12. **Accepted procedures for preparing solutions should be made with** _____ .
*(Average Rigor) (Skill 1.9)*

a. alcohol
b. hydrochloric acid
c. distilled water
d. tap water

**Answer: c. distilled water**

Alcohol and hydrochloric acid should never be used to make solutions unless instructed to do so. All solutions should be made with distilled water as tap water contains dissolved particles which may affect the results of an experiment. The correct answer is (c).

13. **Separating blood into blood cells and plasma involves the process of** _____.
*(Average Rigor) (Skill 1.10)*

a. electrophoresis
b. centrifugation
c. spectrophotometry
d. chromatography

**Answer: b. centrifugation**

Electrophoresis uses electrical charges of molecules to separate them according to their size. Spectrophotometry uses percent light absorbance to measure a color change, thus giving qualitative data a quantitative value. Chromatography uses the principles of capillarity to separate substances. Centrifugation involves spinning substances at a high speed. The more dense part of a solution will settle to the bottom of the test tube, where the lighter material will stay on top. The answer is (c).

14. **Electrophoresis uses electrical charges of molecules to separate them according to their _____.**
    *(Rigorous) (Skill 1.10)*

a. polarization
b. size
c. type
d. shape

**Answer: b. size**

Electrophoresis uses electrical charges of molecules to separate them according to their size. The molecules, such as DNA or proteins, are pulled through a gel toward either the positive end of the gel box or the negative end of the gel box. DNA is negatively charged and moves toward the positive charge. Thus, the answer is (b).

15. **What is specific gravity?**
    *(Average Rigor) (Skill 2.1)*

a. The mass of an object.
b. The ratio of the density of a substance to the density of water.
c. Density.
d. The pull of the earth's gravity on an object.

**Answer: b. The ratio of the density of a substance to the density of water.**

Mass is a measure of the amount of matter in an object. Density is the mass of a substance contained per unit of volume. Weight is the measure of the earth's pull of gravity on an object. The only option here is the ratio of the density of a substance to the density of water, answer (b).

16. **A seltzer tablet changing into bubbles is an example of _____ .**
**(Rigorous) (Skill 2.1)**

a. a physical change
b. a chemical change
c. conversion
d. diffusion

**Answer: b. a chemical change**

A physical change is a change that does not produce a new substance. Conversion is usually used when discussing phase changes of matter, Diffusion occurs in aspects of a mixture when the concentration is equalized. A seltzer tablet changing into bubbles produces a new substance- gas- which is a characteristic of chemical changes. The answer is (b).

17. **When heat is added to most solids, they expand. Why is this the case?**
**(Average Rigor) (Skill 2.2)**

a. The molecules get bigger.
b. The faster molecular motion leads to greater distance between the molecules.
c. The molecules develop greater repelling electric forces.
d. The molecules form a more rigid structure.

**Answer: b. The faster molecular motion leads to greater distance between the molecules.**

The atomic theory of matter states that matter is made up of tiny, rapidly moving particles. These particles move more quickly when warmer, because temperature is a measure of average kinetic energy of the particles. Warmer molecules therefore move further away from each other, with enough energy to separate from each other more often and for greater distances. The individual molecules do not get bigger, by conservation of mass, eliminating answer (a). The molecules do not develop greater repelling electric forces, eliminating answer (c). Occasionally, molecules form a more rigid structure when becoming colder and freezing (such as water)—but this gives rise to the exceptions to heat expansion, so it is not relevant here, eliminating answer
(d). Therefore, the answer is (b).

18.   The relationships between pressure and temperature and between temperature and volume are examples of _____.
   *(Average Rigor) (Skill 2.3)*

a.   indirect variations
b.   direct variations
c.   Boyle's Law
d.   Charles' Law

**Answer:  b.  direct variations**

Charles' Law deals strictly with the relationship between temperature and volume. Boyle's Law deals with the relationship between pressure and volume. These relationships are called direct variations because when one component increases, the other decreases. The answer is (b).

19.   If the volume of a confined gas is increased, what happens to the pressure of the gas? You may assume that the gas behaves ideally, and that temperature and number of gas molecules remain constant.
   *(Rigorous) (Skill 2.3)*

a.   The pressure increases.
b.   The pressure decreases.
c.   The pressure stays the same.
d.   There is not enough information given to answer this question.

**Answer:  b.  The pressure decreases.**

Because we are told that the gas behaves ideally, you may assume that it follows the Ideal Gas Law, i.e. V = nRT/P. This means that an increase in volume must be associated with a decrease in pressure (i.e. higher T means lower P), because we are also given that all the components of the right side of the equation remain constant. Therefore, the answer must be (b).

20. **Vinegar is an example of a _____.**
    *(Easy) (Skill 2.4)*

a. strong acid
b. strong base
c. weak acid
d. weak base

**Answer: c. weak acid**

The main ingredient in vinegar is acetic acid, a weak acid. Vinegar is a useful acid in science classes, because it makes a frothy reaction with bases such as baking soda (e.g. in the quintessential volcano model). Vinegar is not a strong acid, such as hydrochloric acid, because it does not dissociate as fully or cause as much corrosion. It is not a base. Therefore, the answer is (c).

21. **The Law of Conservation of Energy states that _____.**
    *(Easy) (Skill 2.5)*

a. there must be the same number of products and reactants in any chemical equation
b. objects always fall toward large masses such as planets
c. energy is neither created nor destroyed, but may change form
d. lights must be turned off when not in use, by state regulation

**Answer: c. energy is neither created nor destroyed, but may change form.**

Answer (c) is a summary of the Law of Conservation of Energy (for non-nuclear reactions). In other words, energy can be transformed into various forms such as kinetic, potential, electric, or heat energy, but the total amount of energy remains constant. Answer (a) is untrue, as demonstrated by many synthesis and decomposition reactions. Answers (b) and (d) may be sensible, but they are not relevant in this case. Therefore, the answer is (c).

22. **Which of the following is a correct definition for "chemical equilibrium"?**
    *(Average Rigor) (Skill 2.5)*

a. Chemical equilibrium is when the forward and backward reaction rates are equal. The reaction may continue to proceed forward and backward.
b. Chemical equilibrium is when the forward and backward reaction rates are equal, and equal to zero. The reaction does not continue.
c. Chemical equilibrium is when there are equal quantities of reactants and products.
d. Chemical equilibrium is when acids and bases neutralize each other fully.

**Answer:  a.  Chemical equilibrium is when the forward and backward reaction rates are equal. The reaction may continue to proceed forward and backward.**

Chemical equilibrium is defined as when the quantities of reactants and products are at a 'steady state' and are no longer shifting, but the reaction may still proceed forward and backward. The rate of forward reaction must equal the rate of backward reaction. Note that there may or may not be equal amounts of chemicals, and that this is not restricted to a completed reaction or to an acid-base reaction. Therefore, the answer is (a).

23.   **Based on the description of the model of atom below, give the name of the individual(s) who developed the model.**

   **1.  Matter is made up of atoms.**
   **2.  Atoms of an element are similar to each other.**
   **3.  Atoms of different elements are different from each other.**
   **4.  Atoms combine with each other to form new kinds of compounds.**
   *(Rigorous) (Skill 2.6)*

a.   Ernest Rutherford
b.   Neils Bohr
c.   John Dalton
d.   Democritus Thompson


**Answer:  c.  John Dalton**

Democritus was the name of a greek philosopher who developed the first atomic theory of matter. It wasn't until the 1780s that a school teacher expanded on this to create the model with the rules above. Thompson was the last name of a British scientist who (in the late 1800s) first looked in the electrical charge in an atom and developed a model were negative particles were equally mixed in a cloud of positive material. Later experiments by Ernest Rutherford brought about the idea of an atom with a nucleus and orbiting electrons. Neil Bohr refined Rutherford's model into the one that we use today, by stating that electrons have limited stable orbits in which they can be.

24. **What part of an atom has to change to create another isotope of an element?**
    *(Rigorous) (Skill 2.7)*

a.  The number of electrons
b.  The number of neutrons
c.  The arrangement of the electrons
d.  The number of protons

**Answer:  b.  The number of neutrons**

A change in the number of electrons (answer (a)) creates an ion. The change in the arrangement of the electrons (answer (c)), could change the reactivity of an atom temporarily. A change of the number of protons (answer (d)), will change the atom into an ion and/or isotope of another element (this usually only happens in nuclear reactions). Answer (b) is the only one that does not change the relative charge of an atom, while changing the weight of an atom, which in essence is what an isotope is.

25. **The elements in the modern Periodic Table are arranged _____.**
    *(Easy) (Skill 2.8)*

a.  in numerical order by atomic number
b.  randomly
c.  in alphabetical order by chemical symbol
d.  in numerical order by atomic mass

**Answer:  a.  in numerical order by atomic number.**

Although the first periodic tables were arranged by atomic mass, the modern table is arranged by atomic number, i.e. the number of protons in each element. (This allows the element list to be complete and unique.) The elements are not arranged either randomly or in alphabetical order. The answer to this question is therefore (a).

26.    **Which group of metals is the most chemical active?**
       ***(Average Rigor) (Skill 2.8)***

a.    Alkaline earth metals
b.    Transition elements
c.    Alkali metals
d.    Metalloids

**Answer:  c.  Alkali metals**

Answer (d) is the only answer of the four that is not considered one of the metal groups and can thus be dismissed. From right to left on the periodic table the answers would be (c), (a), and then (b), this is also the order of decreasing chemical activity that we see. Thus the answer is (c). An impressive, yet somewhat dangerous demonstration of the Alkali metals activity can be seen by the small explosion that is created when a small amount of pure sodium is dropped into water.

27.    **Which of the following is not a property of metalloids?**
       ***(Rigorous) (Skill 2.9)***

a.    Metalloids are solids at standard temperature and pressure.
b.    Metalloids can conduct electricity to a limited extent.
c.    Metalloids are found in groups 13 through 17.
d.    Metalloids all favor ionic bonding.

**Answer:  d.  Metalloids all favor ionic bonding.**

Metalloids are substances that have characteristics of both metals and nonmetals, including limited conduction of electricity and solid phase at standard temperature and pressure. Metalloids are found in a 'stair-step' pattern from Boron in group 13 through Astatine in group 17. Some metalloids, e.g. Silicon, favor covalent bonding. Others, e.g. Astatine, can bond ionically. Therefore, the answer is (d). Recall that metals/nonmetals/metalloids are not strictly defined by Periodic Table group, so their bonding is unlikely to be consistent with one another.

28. **The electrons in an atom that are used to form a chemical bond are called _____.**
   *(Average Rigor) (Skill 2.10)*

a. outer shell electrons
b. excited electrons
c. valence electrons
d. reactive electrons

**Answer: c. valence electrons**

Answers (a), (b), and (c) could all be used as turns to describe the electrons involved in chemical bonding, depending on the situation. However, only answer (c), valence electrons, is the correct answer because it is the specific name given to these electrons and not a description of the electrons.

29. **Carbon bonds with hydrogen by _____.**
   *(Rigorous) (Skill 2.10)*

a. ionic bonding
b. non-polar covalent bonding
c. polar covalent bonding
d. strong nuclear force

**Answer: c. polar covalent bonding**

Each carbon atom contains four valence electrons, while each hydrogen atom contains one valence electron. A carbon atom can bond with one or more Hydrogen atoms, such that two electrons are shared in each bond. This is covalent bonding, because the electrons are shared. (In ionic bonding, atoms must gain or lose electrons to form ions. The ions are then electrically attracted in oppositely-charged pairs.) Covalent bonds are always polar when between two non-identical atoms, so this bond must be polar. ("polar" means that the electrons are shared unequally, forming a pair of partial charges, i.e. poles.) In any case, the strong nuclear force is not relevant to this problem. The answer to this question is therefore (c).

30. **Which reaction below is a decomposition reaction?**
**(Rigorous) (Skill 2.11)**

a. $HCl + NaOH \rightarrow NaCl + H2O$
b. $C + O2 \rightarrow CO2$
c. $2H2O \rightarrow 2H2 + O2$
d. $CuSO4 + Fe \rightarrow FeSO4 + Cu$

**Answer: c. $2H2O \rightarrow 2H2 + O2$**

To answer this question, recall that a decomposition reaction is one in which there are fewer reactants (on the left) than products (on the right). This is consistent only with answer (c). Meanwhile, note that answer (a) shows a double-replacement reaction (in which two sets of ions switch bonds), answer (b) shows a synthesis reaction (in which there are fewer products than reactants), and answer (d) shows a single-replacement reaction (in which one substance replaces another in its bond, but the other does not get a new bond).

31. **The theory of "sea floor spreading" explains _____.**
**(Average Rigor) (Skill 3.1)**

a. the shapes of the continents
b. how continents collide
c. how continents move apart
d. how continents sink to become part of the ocean floor

**Answer: c. how continents move apart.**

In the theory of "sea floor spreading," the movement of the ocean floor causes continents to spread apart from one another. This occurs because crust plates split apart, and new material is added to the plate edges. This process pulls the continents apart, or may create new separations, and is believed to have caused the formation of the Atlantic Ocean. The answer is (c).

32.  _____ are cracks in the plates of the earth's crust, along which the plates move.
     *(Easy) (Skill 3.2)*

a.  Faults
b.  Ridges
c.  Earthquakes
d.  Volcanoes


**Answer: a. Faults**

Faults are cracks in the earth's crust, and when the earth moves, an earthquake results. Faults may lead to mismatched edges of ground, forming ridges, and ground shape may also be determined by volcanoes. The answer to this question must therefore be (a).


33.  Although Yellowstone has many unique geological features, its entirety is encompassed by one type of geological feature. What is that feature?
     *(Rigorous) (Skill 3.2)*

a.  Caldera
b.  Glacial Trough
c.  Shield Volcano
d.  Laccolith


**Answer: a. Caldera**

Although several times in history glaciers have covered where Yellowstone is currently, they did not create the depression that the park sits in. The other three answers all have to do with magma near the surface at one time or another. A laccolith is created when magma forces its way between two rock layers and creates an obvious dome. Although it is likely that there are laccoliths inside Yellowstone, it is not the feature that contains the whole park. Yellowstone is a volcano; it is not however a shield volcano; it does not constantly have lava flowing out of it. Yellowstone is the site of one of the few known supervolcanoes. At least three times in its history it has exploded, blowing out millions of tons of rock and debris, and creating bowl like depressions known as caldera.

34. Fossils of a dinosaur genus known as *Saurolophus* have been found in both Western North America, and in Mongolia. What is the most likely explanation for these findings?
(Rigorous) (Skill 3.3)

a. Convergent evolution
b. This genus of dinosaurs were powerful swimmers that swam across the Bering Strait.
c. At one time all land masses were conected in a land form known as Pangea, and so the dinsaurs could have easly walked from what is now Mongolia to what is now Western North America.
d. Although Asia and North American were separate continents at the time, low sea levels made it possible for the dinosaurs to walk from one continent to the other.

**Answer: d. Although Asia and North American were separate continents at the time, low sea levels made it possible for the dinosaurs to walk from one continent to the other.**

Convergent evolution can explain how different species have developed similar traits but in this case the fossil record indicates too many similarites, and thus the Saurolophus are a single genus of dinosaurs. (an interesting example of convergent evolution, is that one of the few species other than humans to have distinct fingerprints are Koalas). *Saurolophus* was a land based herbivore with no evidence of strong swimming abilities. As for Pangea, this particular land mass occured roughly 180 million years before the Saurolophus was alive, so it is an unlikely candidate for how evidence of the genus ended up on two continents. This leaves the ability to walk from Asia to North America, and this was accomplished by means of the Bering Land Bridge (where the Bering Strait is now). The Bering Land bridge exsisted because the level of the water in the oceans was lowered by water being stored in large glaciers. This lowering of ocean level was enough to expose what is now the ocean floor between Alaska and Siberia.

35. **The end of a geologic era is most often characterized by _____.**
    *(Average Rigor) (Skill 3.4)*

a.    a general uplifting of the crust
b.    the extinction of the dominant plants and animals
c.    the appearance of new life forms
d.    All of the above


**Answer:  d.  All of the above**

Any of these things can be used to characterize the end of a geologic era, and often a combination of factors are applied to determining the end of an era.


36. **Which of the following is the best explanation of the fundamental concept of Uniformitarianism?**
    *(Rigorous) (Skill 3.4)*

a.    The types and varieties of life between will see a uniform progression over time.
b.    The physical, chemical and biological laws that operate in the geologic past operate in the same way today.
c.    Debris from catastrophic events (i.e. volcanoes, and meteorites) will be evenly distributed over the effected area.
d.    The frequency and intensity of major geologic events will remain consistent over long periods of time.


**Answer:  b.  The physical, chemical and biological laws that operate in the geologic past operate in the same way today.**

While answers (a), (c), and (d) all could represent theories that have been proposed in geology, none of them is an accurate explanation of uniformitarianism. The general idea can be expressed, by the quote, "the present is the key to the past". The forces that we can observe today have been at work over most of Earth's history.

37. **A contour line that has tiny comb-like lines along the inner edge indicates a _____?**
*(Average Rigor) (Skill 3.5)*

a. depression
b. mountain
c. valley
d. river

**Answer: a. depression**

Contour lines are shown as closed circles in elevated areas and as lines with miniature perpendicular lined edges where depressions exist. These little lines are called hachure marks.

38. **Surface ocean currents are caused by which of the following?**
*(Average Rigor) (Skill 3.6)*

a. Earth's rotation.
b. Density changes in water
c. Wind
d. Tidal forces

**Answer: c. Wind**

A current is a large mass of continuously moving oceanic water. Surface ocean currents are mainly wind-driven and occur in all of the world's oceans (example: the Gulf Stream). This is in contrast to deep ocean currents which are driven by changes in density. Surface ocean currents are classified by temperature. Tidal forces cause changes in ocean level however they do not effect surface currents. The Earth's rotation does effect sub-surface ocean currents.

39. **"Neap Tides" are especially weak tides that occur when the Sun and Moon are in a perpindicular arrangment to the Earth, and "Spring Tides" are espically strong tides that occur when the Sun and Moon are in line. At which combination of lunar phases do these tides occur (respectively)?**
*(Rigorous) (Skill 3.6)*

a. Half Moon and Full Moon
b. Quarter Moon and New Moon
c. Gibbous Moon and Quarter Moon
d. Full Moon and New Moon

**Answer: b. Quarter Moon, and New Moon**

"Spring tides" are especially strong tides that occur when the Earth, Sun and Moon are in line, allowing both the Sun and the Moon to exert gravitational force on the Earth and increase tidal bulge height. These tides occur during the full moon and the new moon. "Neap tides" occur during quarter moons, when the sun is illuminating half of the Moon's surface, (the term quarter is used to refer to the fact that the Moon has traveled 1/2 of it's way there its cycle, not the amount of the surface illuminated by the Sun.) A Gibbous Moon describes the Moon between Full and Quarter.

40. **Which of these best decribes the seafloor along the majority of the Pacific shoreline?**
*(Average Rigor) (Skill 3.7)*

a. Continental slope
b. Continental rise
c. Continental shelf
d. Seamount

**Answer: c. Continental shelf**

Usually off the coast of a continent the progression is, the continental shelf, the continental slope, and then the continental rise. A seamount is a term used to describe any volcano that rises at least a kilometer above the seafloor.

41. **Mount Kīlauea, on the island of Hawaii, is a very active volcano that has continuous lava flow into the ocean near it. What is the name of the type of shoreline created at the point where the lava flows meet the water?**
*(Rigorous) (Skill 3.7)*

a. Stacking
b. Submerged
c. Developing
d. Emergent

**Answer: d. Emergent**

Answers (a) and (c) are not technical names for types of shorelines, although a stacked shoreline occurs when an island worn down to rocks. In this case the lava is building on previously deposited lava and although the lava itself is submerging under the water to develop the shoreline the overall effect is the raising of the land out of the water. Thus the correct answer is (d).

42. **The salinity of ocean water is closest to _____ .**
*(Average Rigor) (Skill 3.8)*

a. 0.035 %
b. 0.35 %
c. 3.5 %
d. 35 %

**Answer: c. 3.5 %**

Salinity, or concentration of dissolved salt, can be measured in mass ratio (i.e. mass of salt divided by mass of sea water). For Earth's oceans, the salinity is approximately 3.5 %, or 35 parts per thousand. Note that answers (a) and (d) can be eliminated, because (a) is so dilute as to be hardly saline, while (d) is so concentrated that it would not support ocean life. Therefore, the answer is (c).

43. **Igneous rocks can be classified according to which of the following?** *(Easy) (Skill 3.9)*

a. Texture
b. Composition
c. Formation process
d. All of the above

**Answer: d. All of the above.**

Igneous rocks, which form from the crystallization of molten lava, are classified according to many of their characteristics, including texture, composition, and how they were formed. Therefore, the answer is (d).

44. **Lithification refers to one process to create _____.** *(Rigorous) (Skill 3.9)*

a. metamorphic rocks
b. sedimentary rocks
c. igneous rocks
d. lithium oxide

**Answer: b. sedimentary rocks**

Lithification is the process of sediments coming together to form rocks, i.e. sedimentary rock formation. Metamorphic and igneous rocks are formed via other processes (heat and pressure or volcano, respectively). Lithium oxide shares a word root with "lithification" but is otherwise unrelated to this question. Therefore, the answer must be (b).

45. **Which of these is a true statement about loamy soil?**
    *(Average Rigor) (Skill 3.10)*

a.    Loamy soil is gritty and porous.
b.    Loamy soil is smooth and a good barrier to water.
c.    Loamy soil is hostile to microorganisms.
d.    Loamy soil is velvety and clumpy.

**Answer:  d.  Loamy soil is velvety and clumpy.**

The three classes of soil by texture are: sandy (gritty and porous), clay (smooth, greasy, and most impervious to water), and loamy (velvety, clumpy, and able to hold water and let water flow through). In addition, loamy soils are often the most fertile soils. Therefore, the answer must be (d).

46. **Which of the following is the most accurate definition of a non-renewable resource?**
    *(Average Rigor) (Skill 3.11)*

a.    A nonrenewable resource is never replaced once used.
b.    A nonrenewable resource is replaced on a timescale that is very long relative to human life-spans.
c.    A nonrenewable resource is a resource that can only be manufactured by humans.
d.    A nonrenewable resource is a species that has already become extinct.

**Answer:  b.  A nonrenewable resource is replaced on a timescale that is very long relative to human life-spans.**

Renewable resources are those that are renewed, or replaced, in time for humans to use more of them. Examples include fast-growing plants, animals, or oxygen gas. (Note that while sunlight is often considered a renewable resource, it is actually a nonrenewable but extremely abundant resource.) Nonrenewable resources are those that renew themselves only on very long timescales, usually geologic timescales. Examples include minerals, metals, or fossil fuels. Therefore, the correct answer is (b).

47. **Recently, New Hampshire's famous "Old Man in the Mountain" collapsed. What type of erosion was the principal cause of this? (Rigorous) (Skill 3.12)**

a. Physical weathering
b. Chemical weathering
c. Exfoliation
d. Frost wedging

**Answer:  d.  Frost wedging**

The granite that the "Old Man in the Mountain" was composed of tends to be fairly resislent to the first three types of erosion, however the natural cracks in the cliff face gave plently of places for frost to form and thus widen the cracks. Eventually the widening cracks became to large for the weight of the face to continue to be supported, at which point it collapsed. Even man made attempts to prevent the collapse, which included cables and spikes, were unable to prevent the natural end result of erosion.

48. **A telescope that collects light by using a concave mirror and can produce small images is called a _____. (Easy) (Skill 3.13)**

a. radio telescope
b. reflecting telescope
c. refracting telescope
d. orbital telescope

**Answer:  b.  reflecting telescope**

Reflecting telescopes are commonly used in laboratory settings. Images are produced via the reflection of waves off of a concave mirror. The larger the image produced, the more likely it is to be imperfect. Refracting telscopes use lenses to bend light to focus the image. The term orbital telescope can be used to describe any telescope placed into orbit around Earth, for example the Hubble Space Telescope. A radio telescope monitors background radio emissions from space.

49. **A star's brightness is referred to as its _____.**
    *(Average Rigor) (Skill 3.13)*

a. magnitude
b. mass
c. apparent magnitude
d. intensity

**Answer: a. magnitude**

Magnitude is a measure of a star's brightness. The brighter the object appears, the lower the number value of its magnitude. The apparent magnitude is how bright an observer perceives the object to be. Mass has to do with how much matter can be measured, not brightness. The term intensity is not defined in reference to stars. Researchers may also refer to a stars brightness, in terms of luminosity, which is an absolute value based on the amount of energy the star radiates per second.

50. **Which of the following is the best definition for "meteorite"?**
    *(Easy) (Skill 3.14)*

a. A meteorite is a mineral composed of mica and feldspar.
b. A meteorite is material from outer space, that has struck the earth's surface.
c. A meteorite is an element that has properties of both metals and nonmetals.
d. A meteorite is a very small unit of length measurement.

**Answer: b. A meteorite is material from outer space that has struck the earth's surface.**

Meteoroids are pieces of matter in space, composed of particles of rock and metal. If a meteoroid travels through the earth's atmosphere, friction causes burning and a "shooting star"—i.e. a meteor. If the meteor strikes the earth's surface, it is known as a meteorite. Note that although the suffix –ite often means a mineral, answer (a) is incorrect. Answer (c) refers to a 'metalloid' rather than a 'meteorite', and answer (d) is simply a misleading pun on "meter." Therefore, the answer is (b).

51. **The planet with true retrograde rotation is _____.**
    *(Rigorous) (Skill 3.14)*

a. Pluto
b. Uranus
c. Venus
d. Saturn

**Answer: c. Venus**

Venus has an axial tilt of only 3 degrees and a very slow rotation. It spins in the direction opposite of its counterparts (who spin in the same direction as the Sun). Uranus is also tilted and orbits on its side. However, this is thought to be the consequence of an impact that left the previously prograde rotating planet tilted in such a manner.

52. **Earth's galaxy is found in the Milky Way. What kind of galaxy is it?**
    *(Average Rigor) (Skill 3.15)*

a. Irregular
b. Elliptical
c. Conical
d. Spiral

**Answer: d. Spiral**

An irregular galaxy has no real structured appearance; they are in their early stages of life. An elliptical galaxy is smooth ellipses, containing little dust and and gas, but composed of millions or trillions of stars. Spiral galaxies are disk-shaped and have extending arms that rotate around its dense center. Earth's galaxy is a spiral galaxy.

53.     **What is the main difference between the "condensation hypothesis" and the "tidal hypothesis" for the origin of the solar system?**
*(Rigorous) (Skill 3.16)*

a.      The tidal hypothesis can be tested, but the condensation hypothesis cannot.

b.      The tidal hypothesis proposes a near collision of two stars pulling on each other, but the condensation hypothesis proposes condensation of rotating clouds of dust and gas.

c.      The tidal hypothesis explains how tides began on planets such as Earth, but the condensation hypothesis explains how water vapor became liquid on Earth.

d.      The tidal hypothesis is based on Aristotelian physics, but the condensation hypothesis is based on Newtonian mechanics.


**Answer:  b.  The tidal hypothesis proposes a near collision of two stars pulling on each other, but the condensation hypothesis proposes condensation of rotating clouds of dust and gas.**

Most scientists believe in the "condensation hypothesis," which states that the solar system began when rotating clouds of dust and gas condensed into the sun and planets. A minority opinion is the "tidal hypothesis," i.e. that the sun almost collided with a large star. The large star's gravitational field would have then pulled gases out of the sun; these gases are thought to have begun to orbit the sun and condense into planets. Because both of these hypotheses deal with ancient, unrepeatable events, neither can be tested, eliminating answer (a). Note that both 'tidal' and 'condensation' have additional meanings in physics, but those are not relevant here, eliminating answer (c). Both hypotheses are based on best guesses using modern physics, eliminating answer (d).  Therefore, the answer is (b).

54. **What are the most significant and prevalent elements in the biosphere?**
*(Easy) (Skill 3.17)*

a. Carbon, hydrogen, oxygen, nitrogen, phosphorus
b. Carbon, hydrogen, sodium, iron, calcium
c. Carbon, oxygen, sulfur, manganese, iron
d. Carbon, hydrogen, oxygen, nickel, sodium, nitrogen

**Answer: a. Carbon, hydrogen, oxygen, nitrogen, phosphorus**

Organic matter (and life as we know it) is based on carbon atoms, bonded to hydrogen and oxygen. Nitrogen and phosphorus are the next most significant elements, followed by sulfur and then trace nutrients such as iron, sodium, calcium, and others. Therefore, the answer is (a). If you know that the formula for any carbohydrate contains carbon, hydrogen, and oxygen, that will help you narrow the choices to (a) and (d) in any case.

55. **What makes up the largest abiotic portion of the nitrogen cycle?**
*(Average Rigor) (Skill 3.17)*

a. Nitrogen fixing bacteria
b. Nitrates
c. Decomposers
d. Atmosphere

**Answer: d. Atomsphere**

Since answers (a) and (c) are both examples of living organisms, they are biotic components of the nitrogen cycle. Nitrates are one type of nitrogen compond, (making it abiotic) that can be found in soil and in living organisms; however, it makes up a small portion of the available nitrogen. The atmosphere being 78% nitrogen gas (an abiotic component) makes up the largest source available to the nitrogen cycle.

56. **Which type of cloud is most likely to produce precipitation?**
   *(Average Rigor) (Skill 3.18)*

a. Cirrocumulus
b. Stratocumulus
c. Cumulonimbus
d. Cirrostratus

**Answer: c. Cumulonimbus**

Cirrocumulus and cirrostratus clouds (answers (a) and (d)) occur at the highest levels of cloud formation, and are thin veil like or small patches, respectively. Stratocumulus clouds (answer (b)), occur low in the atmosphere, and are usually large irregular shaped puffs with large amounts of blue sky, these are the clouds that are usually used when looking for shapes in clouds. Leaving cumulonimbus clouds (answer (c)) to be correct. These clouds are most often associated with thunderstorms, these large, puffy, clouds have smooth or flattened tops, and can produce heavy rain and thunder.

57. **Air moving northward from the horse latitudes produces a belt of winds called the _____.**
   *(Rigorous) (Skill 3.18)*

a. Prevailing westerlies
b. North westerlies
c. Trade winds
d. Prevailing Easterlies

**Answer: a. Prevailing westerlies**

The prevailing westerlies are the winds found in the middle latitudes between 30 and 60 degrees latitude. They blow from the high pressure area in the horse latitudes towards the poles.

58. **Moss and lichen are found within polar ice in which climate?**
    *(Average Rigor) (Skill 3.19)*

a. Taiga
b. Grasslands
c. Tundra
d. Rainforests

**Answer: c. Tundra**

The tundra's climate is quite cold, causing moss and lichen to be found in the fragile polar ice. The climate in the rain forests are tropical, taiga is a mild climate, neither extremely hot nor extremely cold, and the climate in grasslands must be mild in order to support the deep root systems.

59. **Which is a form of precipitation?**
    *(Rigorous) (Skill 3.20)*

a. Snow
b. Frost
c. Fog
d. All of the above

**Answer: a. Snow**

Snow is a form of precipitation. Precipitation is the product of the condensation of atmospheric water vapor that falls to the Earth's surface. It occurs when the atmosphere becomes saturated with water vapor and the water condenses and falls out of solution. Frost and fog do not qualify as precipitates.

60. **When water falls to a cave floor and evaporates, it may deposit calcium carbonate. This process leads to the formation of which of the following?**
    *(Easy) (Skill 3.21)*

a.  Stalactites
b.  Stalagmites
c.  Fault lines
d.  Sedimentary rocks

**Answer: b.  Stalagmites**

To answer this question, recall the trick to remember the kinds of crystals formed in caves. Stalactites have a 't' in them, because they form hanging from the ceiling resembling a 't'). Stalagmites have an 'm' in them, because they make bumps on the floor (resembling an 'm'). Note that fault lines and sedimentary rocks are irrelevant to this question. Therefore, the answer must be (b).

61. **Quicksand is created by the Interaction of very fine sand and water. The process that creates quicksand is called _____.**
    *(Rigorous) (Skill 3.21)*

a.  absorption
b.  percolation
c.  leaching
d.  runoff

**Answer: b.  percolation**

Quicksand is created when ground water is forced up through sandy soil, creating a semiliquid state. Percolation refers to this movement of water through the sand. If absorption had been the answer, then beach sand, rather than being good for making sand castles, would take out an untold number of tourists daily. Leaching is the absorption of soluble compounds from the ground. Leaching is the principle method of groundwater contamination. Runoff is as simple as it sounds, the water that flows over the ground before reaching some form of surface water.

62. **What is the source for most of the United States' drinking water?**
    **(Rigorous) (Skill 3.22)**

a.    Desalinated ocean water
b.    Surface water (lakes, streams, mountain runoff)
c.    Rainfall into municipal reservoirs
d.    Groundwater

**Answer:  d.  Groundwater**

Groundwater currently provides drinking water for 53% of the population of the United States. (Although groundwater is often less polluted than surface water, it can be contaminated and it is very hard to clean once it is polluted. If too much groundwater is used from one area, then the ground may sink or shift, or local salt water may intrude from ocean boundaries.) The other answer choices can be used for drinking water, but they are not the most widely used. Therefore, the answer is (d).

63. **Contamination may enter groundwater by _____.**
    **(Easy) (Skill 3.23)**

a.    air pollution
b.    leaking septic tanks
c.    photochemical processes
d.    sewage treatment plants.

**Answer:  b.  leaking septic tanks**

Leaking septic tanks allow contamination to slowly seep into the ground, where it is absorbed into the water table and infects the groundwater. The only other reasonable possibility is sewage treatment plants, which isolate the waste from ground water until it has reached a state that it will not be hazardous to release into ground or surface water.

64. **Which of the following is not a common type of acid in "acid rain" or acidified surface water?**
    *(Average Rigor) (Skill 3.24)*

a.  Nitric acid
b.  Sulfuric acid
c.  Carbonic acid
d.  Hydrofluoric acid

**Answer: d. Hydrofluoric acid**

Acid rain forms predominantly from pollutant oxides in the air (usually nitrogen-based NOx or sulfur-based SOx), which become hydrated into their acids (nitric or sulfuric acid). Because of increased levels of carbon dioxide pollution, carbonic acid is also common in acidified surface water environments. Hydrofluoric acid can be found, but it is much less common. In general, carbon, nitrogen, and sulfur are much more prevalent in the environment than fluorine. Therefore, the answer is (d).

65. **Identify the correct sequence of organization of living things from lower to higher order:**
    *(Average Rigor) (Skill 4.1)*

a.  Cell, organelle, organ, tissue, system, organism.
b.  Cell, tissue, organ, organelle, system, organism.
c.  Organelle, cell, tissue, organ, system, organism.
d.  Organelle, tissue, cell, organ, system, organism.

**Answer: c. Organelle, cell, tissue, organ, system, organism.**

Organelles are parts of the cell; cells make up tissue, which makes up organs. Organs work together in systems (e.g. the respiratory system), and the organism is the living thing as a whole. Therefore, the answer must be (c).

66. **Which of the following is not a necessary characteristic of living things?**
    *(Average Rigor) (Skill 4.2)*

a.  Movement
b.  Reduction of local entropy
c.  Ability to cause change in local energy form
d.  Reproduction

**Answer:  a. Movement.**

There are many definitions of "life," but in all cases, a living organism reduces local entropy, changes chemical energy into other forms, and reproduces. Not all living things move, however, so the correct answer is (a).

67. **Which of the following is not one of the principles of Darwin's ideas of natural selection?**
    *(Average Rigor) (Skill 4.3)*

a.  More individuals are produced than will survive
b.  The Individuals in a certain species vary from generation to generation
c.  Only the fittest members of a species survive
d.  Some genes allow for better survival of an animal

**Answer:  c. Only the fittest members of a species survive.**

Answers (a), (b) and (d) were all specifically noted by Darwin in his hypotheses. Answer (c) is often misquoted to represent this particular theory, but was not mentioned by Darwin himself.

68. **What is the principle driving force for evolution of antibiotic resistant bacteria?**
    *(Rigorous) (Skill 4.3)*

a.     Mutation
b.     Reproduction method
c.     Population size
d.     Emigration

**Answer: c. Population size**

Most bacteria reproduce asexually, thus there is not a contribution to the variabilty of the population, thus answer (b) is not the driving force. Answer (d) emigration, or the act of moving away from an area usually occurs after a bacteria has developed a resistance and not before. Mutation, answer (a), is a critical aspect in the evolution of antibiotic resistant bacteria, however useful mutations happen rarely and thus alone would be unlikely to develop a strain of antibiotic resistent bacteria. Only a large population size, answer (c), and the ability to quickly build that population would make it likely that a member of the colony would have devloped a useful mutation.

69. **What cell organelle contains the cell's stored food?**
    *(Rigorous) (Skill 4.4)*

a.     Vacuoles
b.     Golgi Apparatus
c.     Ribosomes
d.     Lysosomes

**Answer: a. Vacuoles**

In a cell, the sub-parts are called organelles. Of these, the vacuoles hold stored food (and water and pigments). The Golgi apparatus sorts molecules from other parts of the cell; the ribosomes are sites of protein synthesis; the lysosomes contain digestive enzymes. This is consistent only with answer (a).

70. **The first stage of mitosis is called _____.**
    *(Average Rigor) (Skill 4.5)*

a.  telophase
b.  anaphase
c.  prophase
d.  mitophase

**Answer: c. prophase**

In mitosis, the division of somatic cells, prophase is the stage where the cell enters mitosis. The four stages of mitosis, in order, are: prophase, metaphase, anaphase, and telophase. ("mitophase" is not one of the steps.) During prophase, the cell begins the nonstop process of division. Its chromatin condenses, its nucleolus disappears, the nuclear membrane breaks apart, mitotic spindles form, its cytoskeleton breaks down, and centrioles push the spindles apart. Note that interphase, the stage where chromatin is loose, chromosomes are replicated, and cell metabolism is occurring, is technically not a stage of mitosis; it is a precursor to cell division.

71. **Which process result in a haploid chromosome number?**
    *(Rigorous) (Skill 4.5)*

a.  Mitosis
b.  Meiosis I
c.  Meiosis II
d.  Neither mitosis nor meiosis

**Answer: c. Meiosis II.**

Meiosis is the division of sex cells. The resulting chromosome number is half the number of parent cells, i.e. a 'haploid chromosome number'. Meiosis I mirrors mitosis, resulting in diploid cells. It is only during meiosis II that the number of chromosomes is halved. Mitosis, however, is the division of other cells, in which the chromosome number is the same as the parent cell chromosome number. Therefore, the answer is (b).

72. **Klinefelter Syndrome is a condition in which a person is born with two X chromosomes and one Y chromosome. What process during meiosis would cause this to happen?**
    *(Rigorous) (Skill 4.6)*

a.  Inversion
b.  Translocation
c.  Nondisjunction
d.  Arrangement failure

**Answer: c. Nondisjunction**

Nondisjunction describes the process by which chromosomes (or chromatids) fail to separate, and one cell (in this case gamette) recieves both copies and the other cell receives none. Inversion is a process where a gene reverses itself wit in the chromosome. Translocation can lead to some gentic disorders, because a portion of one chromosome is swapped with a portion of another chromosome. As a term arrangement failure might be a good description for a number of genetic processes (including non-disjunction) but does not have a specifc meaning itself.

73. **Animal cells differ from plant cells because they have _____.**
    *(Average Rigor) (Skill 4.7)*

a.  vacuoles
b.  hair cells
c.  epidermal cells
d.  centrioles

**Answer: d. centrioles**

All cells have vacuoles. Both plant and animal cells have hair cells and epidermal cells. The primary difference between animal cells and plant cells is that animal cells have centrioles.

74.    **In the Law of Dominance _____.**
       *(Easy) (Skill 4.8)*

a.    only one of the two possible alleles from each parent is passed on to the offspring
b.    alleles sort independently of each other
c.    one trait may cover up the allele of the other trait
d.    flowers have white alleles and purple alleles


**Answer:  c.  one trait may cover up the allele of the other trait.**

Alleles sort independently of one another in the Law of Independent Assortment; The Law of Segregation states that only one of the two possible alleles from each parent is passed on to the offspring. The color of flower alleles has nothing to do with any particular laws of inheritance. The answer is (c). The Law of Dominance says that in a pair of alleles, one trait may cover up the allele of the other trait.


75.    **A white flower is crossed with a red flower. Which of the following is a sign of incomplete dominance?**
       *(Average Rigor) (Skill 4.8)*

a.    Pink flowers
b.    Red flowers
c.    White flowers.
d.    No flowers


**Answer:  a.  Pink flowers**

Incomplete dominance means that neither the red nor the white gene is strong enough to suppress the other. Therefore both are expressed, leading in this case to the formation of pink flowers. Therefore, the answer is (a).

76.	A carrier of a genetic disorder is heterozygous for a disorder that is recessive in nature. Hemophilia is a sex-linked disorder. What does this mean?
	*(Easy) (Skill 4.9)*

a.	Only females can be carriers.
b.	Only males can be carriers.
c.	Both males and females can be carriers.
d.	Neither females nor males can be carriers.

**Answer:  a.  Only females can be carriers.**

Since hemophilia is a sex-linked disorder the gene only appears on the X chromosome, with no counterpart on the Y chromosome. Since males are XY they cannot be heterozygous for the trait, what ever is on the single X chromosome will be expressed. Females being XX can be heterozygous. Answer (c) would describe a genetic disorder that is recessive and expressed on one of the somatic chromosomes (not sex-linked). Answer (d) would describe a genetic disorder that is dominant and expressed on any of the chromosomes. An example of answer (c) is sickle cell anemia. An example of answer (d) is achondroplasia (the most common type of short-limbed dwarfism), in fact for this condition, people that are homozygous dominant for the gene that creates the disorder usually have severe health problems if they live past infancy, so almost all individuals with this disorder are carriers.

77.	An Arabic horse's purebred bloodline makes it a good example of
	_____.
	*(Rigorous) (Skill 4.9)*

a.	a homozygous animal
b.	a heterozygous animal
c.	codominance
d.	a poly-genic character

**Answer:  a.  A homozygous animal**

A heterozygous animal is a hybrid. Codominance occurs when the genes form new phenotypes. A polygenic character is when many alleles code for one phenotype. A homozygous animal is a purebred, having two of the same genes present, as in a purebred horse breed. The answer is (a).

78. **Which of the following is not a nucleotide?**
    *(Average Rigor) (Skill 4.10)*

a. Adenine
b. Alanine
c. Cytosine
d. Guanine

**Answer: b. Alanine**

Alanine is an amino acid. Adenine, cytosine, guanine, thymine, and uracil are nucleotides. The correct answer is (b).

79. **Amino acids are carried to the ribosome in protein synthesis by** _____.
    *(Rigorous) (Skill 4.10)*

a. transfer RNA (tRNA)
b. transport enzymes
c. ribosomal RNA (rRNA)
d. cytoskeletal transport proteins

**Answer: a. transfer RNA (tRNA)**

The function of tRNA is to carry and position amino acids to/on the ribosomes. mRNA copies DNA code and brings it to the ribosomes; rRNA is in the ribosome itself. Although there are enzymes and proteins, both attached and not attached to the cell's cytoskeleton, neither transport individual amino acids to the ribosome. Thus, the answer is (a).

80. **Which of the following features is/are found in eukaryotic cells but not in prokaryotic cells?**
    1. **Nucleus**
    2. **Mitochondria**
    3. **Cytoskeleton**
    4. **Vacules**
    *(Easy) (Skill 4.11)*

a.  4 Only
b.  1 and 2
c.  1, 2 and 4
d.  1, 2 and 3

**Answer:  d.  1, 2 and 3**

All cells contain vacuoles, which may serve a diverse number of purposes depending on the cell.  The other three items can be found in all eukaryotic cells.

81. **Which of the following is not a member of Kingdom Fungi?**
    *(Easy) (Skill 4.12)*

a.  Mold
b.  Blue-green algae
c.  Mildew
d.  Mushrooms

**Answer:  b.  Blue-green algae.**

Mold (a), mildew (c), and mushrooms (d) are all types of fungus. Blue-green algae, however, is in Kingdom Eubacteria.  Therefore, the answer is (b).

82. Diatoms are one of the primary contributors to photosynethis in the oceans. They also have a unique cell wall made up of silicate, which often makes them sink in the water. Although some diatoms might form colonies most are single celled. Diatoms are usually nonmotile, although in many species the gametes have flagella. Based on this information which answer is the best identification of diatoms. *(Rigorous) (Skill 4.12)*

a. Protozoans
b. Euglenas
c. Protists
d. Blue-Green Algae

**Answer: c. Protists**

Euglena is a species of protozoan that uses a flagella to move, but like all protozoans, they have chloroplasts and can preform photosynthesis. Although like diatoms, Blue-green algae does use photosynthesis; the mechanism is considerably different, not relying on chloroplasts as in dlatoms. Blue-green alae are bacteria, which means that they will not have a cell wall, as a dlatom does. Being a (usually) single cellular eukaroytic organism capable of photosynthesis means that the only one of the descriptors that is broad enough to include diatoms is Protist. An interesting side note: a large portion of beach sand is made up of old diatom silicate cell walls.

83. **Extensive use of antibacterial soap has been found to increase the virulence of certain infections in hospitals. Which of the following might be an explanation for this phenomenon?**
    *(Average Rigor) (Skill 4.13)*

a. Antibacterial soaps do not kill viruses.
b. Antibacterial soaps do not incorporate the same antibiotics used as medicine.
c. Antibacterial soaps kill a lot of bacteria, and only the hardiest ones survive to reproduce.
d. Antibacterial soaps can be very drying to the skin.

**Answer: c. Antibacterial soaps kill a lot of bacteria, and only the hardiest ones survive to reproduce.**

All of the answer choices in this question are true statements, but the question specifically asks for a cause of increased disease virulence in hospitals. This phenomenon is due to natural selection. The bacteria that can survive contact with antibacterial soap are the strongest ones, and without other bacteria competing for resources, they have more opportunity to flourish. This problem has led to several antibiotic-resistant bacterial diseases in hospitals nationwide. Therefore, the answer is (c). However, note that answers (a) and (d) may be additional problems with over-reliance on antibacterial products.

84. **Which part of a plant is responsible for transporting water?**
    *(Easy) (Skill 4.14)*

a. Phloem
b. Xylem
c. Stomata
d. Cortex

**Answer: b. Xylem**

The xylem transport a plants food. Stomata are openings on the underside of a leaf that allows for the passage of carbon dioxide, oxygen and water. The Cortex is where a plant stores food. So the only answer is (b) the xylem, which is where water is transported up the plant.

85.     **Which plant tissues contain chloroplasts?**
        *(Average Rigor) (Skill 4.14)*

a.      Stomata
b.      Palisade mesophyll
c.      Spongy Mesophyll
d.      Endosperm

**Answer:  b.  Palisade mesophyll**

Palisade mesophyll is one part of the leaf, in this case the part where chloroplasts exist and photosynthesis occurs. The spongy mesophyll is the other part of the leaf, where gas exchange occurs. The stomata are the parts of the leaf that are the openings for air to enter and exit the leaf. The endosperm is the food source in the seed.

86.     **As in all processess, plant growth must deal with the Law of Conservation of Mass and Energy. Most people recongize the Sun as the source of a plant's energy, however, what is the primary source of the introduction of mass?**
        *(Rigorous) (Skill 4.15)*

a.      Water absorbed through the roots.
b.      Nutrient's and minerals absorbed through the roots.
c.      Carbon absorbed through the roots.
d.      Carbon absorbed through the stomata.

**Answer:  d.  Carbon absorbed through the stomata.**

Although water, nutrients, and minerals are absorbed through the roots by a plant, they do not make up the bulk of the added mass when a plant grows. Most of the added mass during plant growth is in the form of organic compounds, meaning the plant needs a large source of carbon to grow. Carbon dioxide taken in by the plant when it opens, its stomata is usually turned into glucose by photosynthesis. This glucose can then be either metabolized for energy or altered to form the other orgnaic compounds the plant requires.

87.    **Which of the following organisms use spores to reproduce?**
       **_(Average Rigor) (Skill 4.16)_**

a.    Fish
b.    Flowering plants
c.    Conifers
d.    Ferns


**Answer:  d.  Ferns**

Ferns, in Division Pterophyta, reproduce with spores and flagellated sperm.
Flowering plants reproduce via seeds, and conifers reproduce via seeds
protected in cones (e.g. pinecone). Fish, of course, reproduce sexually.
Therefore, the answer is (d).


88.    **Which of the following is not characteristic of gymnosperms?**
       **_(Rigorous) (Skill 4.16)_**

a.    They are less dependent on water to assist in reproduction than other
      plant groups.
b.    Gymnosperms have cones which protect their seeds.
c.    Gymnosperms reproduce asexually.
d.    Gymnosperm seeds and pollen are easily carried by the wind.


**Answer:  c.  Gymnosperms reproduce asexually.**

Gymnosperms (which means naked seeds) were the first plants to evolve with
seeds. They are less dependent on water to assist in reproduction, and their
seeds are transported by wind. Pollen from the male is also carried by the wind.
Thus, gymnosperms cannot be asexual, which makes (c) the correct answer.

89. **Mollusca have an open circulatory system. Their sinuses serve which purposes?**
    *(Rigorous) (Skill 4.17)*

a.  Breathing
b.  Bathing
c.  Filtering food
d.  Circulating blood

**Answer: b. Bathing**

Creatures in the Mollusca genus include clams, octupi, and soft bodied animals, which have a muscular foot for movement. Most of these creatures breathe through gills. With the open circulatory system, the sinuses are for bathing the body regions of the creature.

90. **Which is the correct sequence of insect development?**
    *(Easy) (Skill 4.18)*

a.  Egg, pupa, larva, adult
b.  Egg, larva, pupa, adult
c.  Egg, adult, larva, pupa
d.  Pupa, egg, larva, adult

**Answer: b. Egg, larva, pupa, adult.**

An insect begins as an egg, hatches into a larva (e.g. caterpillar), forms a pupa (e.g. cocoon), and emerges as an adult (e.g. moth). Therefore, the nswer is (b).

91.     **The two strands of a DNA molecule are held together by what kind of bond?**
        *(Average Rigor) (Skill 4.18)*

a.      Polar-covalent
b.      Ionic
c.      Non-polar Covalent
d.      Hydrogen

**Answer: d. Hydrogen**

If covalent bonding (polar or non-polar) was used to join the strands of DNA together, the bonds would require a great deal of energy to separate, making transcription and copying difficult. Ionic bonds are not stable enough in solution to maintain the double helix. Hydrogen bonds form between the complementary base pair in the DNA, 2 bonds for adenine and thymine, and 3 bonds between cytosine and guanine.

92.     **Many male birds sing long complicated songs that describe their identity and the area of land that they claim. Which of the answers below is the best decription of this behavior?**
        *(Rigorous) (Skill 4.19)*

a.      Innate territorial behavior
b.      Learned competitve behavior
c.      Innate mating behavior
d.      Learned territorial behavior

**Answer: d. Learned territorial behavior**

Birds often learn their songs, through a combination of trial and error, and listening to the songs of other members of their species (in some cases other species, this is called mimicry). Thus answers (a) and (c) are not correct. Typically a male bird will use a short song to impress a mate; the longer song is territorial because it is trying to convey to other males both identity, and the territory that it claims.

93. **Echinodermata are best known for what characteristic?**
(*Average Rigor*) (*Skill 4.20*)

a.  Their slimy skin
b.  Their Dry Habitat
c.  Their tube feet
d.  Their tentacles.

**Answer:  c.  Their tube feet**

Echinodermata include sea urchins and starfish. They live in marine habitats, have spiny skin, and do not have tentacles. Thus, the best known characteristic choice here would have to be their tube feet, which they use for locomotion and feeding.

94. **Which of the following animals are most likely to live in a tropical rain forest?**
(*Easy*) (*Skill 4.21*)

a.  Reindeer
b.  Monkeys
c.  Puffins
d.  Bears

**Answer:  b.  Monkeys**

The tropical rainforest biome is hot and humid, and is very fertile—it is thought to contain almost half of the world's species. Reindeer (a), puffins (c), and bears (d), however, are usually found in much colder climates. There are several species of monkeys that thrive in hot, humid climates, so answer (b) is correct.

95.  **Which one of the following biomes makes up the greatest percentage of the biosphere?**
     *(Rigorous) (Skill 4.21)*

a.  Desert
b.  Tropical rainforest
c.  Marine
d.  Temperate deciduous forest

**Answer: c. Marine**

All land biomes, which includes answers (a), (b), and (d) make up approximately 25% of the earth's surface, leaving the other 75% to the marine biome. Additionally the marine biome can range in depth from the air above the water, to several miles in depth. This combined make answer (c) the correct answer.

96.  **Which of the following terms does not describe a way that the human race has had a negative impact on the biosphere?**
     *(Rigorous) (Skill 4.22)*

a.  Biological magnification
b.  Pollution
c.  Carrying capacity
d.  Simplifcation of the food web

**Answer: c. Carrying capacity**

Most people recognize the harmful effects that pollution has caused, especially air pollution and the concept of Global Warming. Pollution, and regular use of pesticides and herbicides introduce toxins in the food web, biological magnification relates to how the concentration of these toxins increases the farther you move away from the source, so that animals at the top of the food chain, for example bald eagles, develop dangerous levels of toxins, and maybe responsible for declining birth rates in some species. Simplification of the food web has to do with a small variety of farming crops replacing large habitats, and thus shrinking or destroying some ecosystems. Carrying capacity, on the other hand, is simply a term that relates amount of life a certain habitat can sustain. It is term independent of human action, so the answer is (c). This is not to say that the number of humans is not having an impact; we are overpopulating the planet; in doing so, we are moving past the carrying capacity of many habitats.

97.    Multiple sclerosis is an autoimmune disease that prevents nerves that are being attacked from being properly insulated, thus preventing normal propagation of the nerve signal. Which part of the nervous system is the most likely target of the body's immune system in this diease?
*(Rigorous) (Skill 4.23)*

a.    Axon
b.    Synapse
c.    Dendrite
d.    Myelin


**Answer:  d.  Myelin**

Answers (a), (b), and (c) are all part of the neuron, and although they all play a part in propagating a nerve impulse, only the myelin shealth composed of Schwann cells insulates these parts of the neuron. It is possible that in later stages of multiple sclerosis there will be damage to axons. This will usually only happen after the myelin sheath has been stripped away.


98.    Which of the following is not a way in which alcohol, drugs, or tobacco affect the normal processes of the human body?
*(Average Rigor) (Skill 4.24)*

a.    Absorption of nutrients
b.    Interference with physical and mental development
c.    Damaging developing organs
d.    Boosting the immune system


**Answer:  d.  Boosting the immune system**

Depending on the substance, alcohol, drugs, and tobacco are all toxic items in the human body. They can slow down or speed up the absorption of nutrients, can have devastating affect on the development of mental and physical processes, and their effect on developing organs can cause major diseases such as bronchitis and asthma. The one thing they do not do, despite wishful thinking, is to positively effect the body by boosting the immune system.

99. **Water inside a closed vessel is in thermal equilibrium in all three states (ice, water, and vapor) at 273.15° in what measurement scale?**
*(Average Rigor) (Skill 5.1)*

a. Farenheit
b. Celsius
c. BTU (British Thermal Unit)
d. Kelvin

**Answer: d. Kelvin**

The BTU is not a measure of temperature, it is a measure of work. The other three scales are different because they are set for different zero points. The zero point for Kelvin is absolute zero. A sealed glass of ice water, at 273.15° Kelvin, contains ice, water, and water vapor, as this is the freezing temperature of water on the Kelvin scale.

100. **The transfer of heat by electromagnetic waves is called _____.**
*(Easy) (Skill 5.2)*

a. conduction
b. convection
c. phase change
d. radiation

**Answer: d. radiation**

Heat transfer via electromagnetic waves (which can occur even in a vacuum) is called radiation. (Heat can also be transferred by direct contact (conduction), by fluid current (convection), and by matter changing phase, but these are not relevant here.) The answer to this question is therefore (d).

101. **When you step out of the shower, the floor feels colder on your feet than the bathmat. Which of the following is the correct explanation for this phenomenon?**
**(Rigorous) (Skill 5.2)**

a. The floor is colder than the bathmat.
b. The bathmat being smaller that the floor quickly reaches equilibrium with your body temperature.
c. Heat is conducted more easily into the floor.
d. Water is absorbed from your feet into the bathmat so it doesn't evaporate as quickly as it does off the floor thus not cooling the bathmat as quickly.

**Answer: c. Heat is conducted more easily into the floor.**

When you step out of the shower and onto a surface, the surface is most likely at room temperature, regardless of its composition (eliminating answer (a)). The bathmat is likely a good insulator and is unlikely to reach equilibrium with your body temperature after a short exposure so answer (b) is incorrect. Although evaporation does have a cooling effect, it the short time it takes you to step from the bathmat to the floor, it is unlikely to have a significant effect on the floor temperature (eliminating answer (d)). Your feet feel cold when heat is transferred from them to the surface, which happens more easily on a hard floor than a soft bathmat. This is because of differences in specific heat (the energy required to change temperature, which varies by material). Therefore, the answer must be (c), i.e. heat is conducted more easily into the floor from your feet.

102. **Energy is measured with the same units as _____.**
**(Average Rigor) (Skill 5.3)**

a. force
b. momentum
c. work
d. power

**Answer: c. work**

In SI units, energy is measured in Joules, i.e. (mass)(length squared)/(time squared). This is the same unit as is used for work. You can verify this by calculating that since work is force times distance, the units work out to be the same. Force is measured in Newtons in SI; momentum is measured in (mass)(length)/(time); power is measured in Watts (which equal Joules/second). Therefore, the answer must be (c).

**103.** **A boulder sitting on the edge of a cliff has which type of energy?** *(Easy) (Skill 5.4)*

a.    Kinetic energy
b.    Latent energy
c.    No energy
d.    Potential energy

**Answer:  d.  Potential energy**

Answer (a) would be true if the boulder fell off the cliff and started falling. Answer (c) would be a difficult condition to find since it would mean that no outside forces where operating on an object, and gravity is difficult to avoid. Answer (b) might be a good description of answer (d) which is the correct energy. The boulder has potential energy is imparted from the force of gravity.

**104.** **Newton's Laws are taught in science classes because _____.** *(Rigorous) (Skill 5.4)*

a.    they are the correct analysis of inertia, gravity, and forces
b.    they are a close approximation to correct physics, for usual Earth conditions
c.    they accurately incorporate relativity  into studies of forces
d.    Newton was a well-respected scientist in his time

**Answer:  b.  They are a close approximation to correct physics, for usual Earth conditions.**

Although Newton's Laws are often taught as fully correct for inertia, gravity, and forces, it is important to realize that Einstein's work (and that of others) has indicated that Newton's Laws are reliable only at speeds much lower than that of light. This is reasonable, though, for most middle- and high-school applications. At speeds close to the speed of light, Relativity considerations must be used. Therefore, the only correct answer is (b).

105. **Which of the following is a correct explanation for an astronaut's "weightlessness"?**
*(Average Rigor) (Skill 5.5)*

a.   Astronauts continue to feel the pull of gravity in space, but they are so far from planets that the force is small.
b.   Astronauts continue to feel the pull of gravity in space, but spacecraft have such powerful engines that those forces dominate, reducing effective weight.
c.   Astronauts do not feel the pull of gravity in space, because space is a vacuum.
d.   The cumulative gravitational forces, that the astronaut is experiencing, from all sources in the solar system equal out to a net gravitational force of zero.

**Answer:  a.  Astronauts continue to feel the pull of gravity in space, but they are so far from planets that the force is small.**

Gravity acts over tremendous distances in space (theoretically, infinite distance, though certainly at least as far as any astronaut has traveled). However, gravitational force is inversely proportional to distance squared from a massive body. This means that when an astronaut is in space, s/he is far enough from the center of mass of any planet that the gravitational force is very small, and s/he feels 'weightless'. Space is mostly empty (i.e. vacuum), and spacecraft do have powerful engines. However, none of these has the effect attributed to it in the incorrect answer choices (b), or (c). Although, theoretically there is a point in space where the cumulative gravitational forces of sources within the solar system would equal a net force of zero, that point would be in constant motion and difficult to find, making answer (d) unlikely at best and but more accurately near impossible to keep an astronaught at this point. The answer to this question must therefore be (a).

106. The picture shows a view from slightly above of a teacher swinging a yo-yo over their head. The teacher would be holding onto the string in the center of the circle, and the circle itself describeds the path of the yo-yo. Arrows 1,2 and 3 describe the forces on the yo-yo. Which answer below names the forces correctly?
*(Rigorous) (Skill 5.5)*

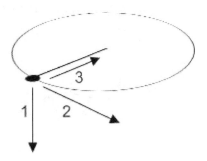

a.   1 is inertia, 2 is centripetal force, 3 is graviy
b.   1 is centripedal force, 2 is gravity, 3 is inertia
c.   1 is gravity, 2 is inertia, 3 is centripetal
d.   1 is gravity, 2 is inertia, 3 is centrifugal

**Answer: c. 1 is gravity, 2 is inertia, 3 is centripetal**

Althrough the yo-yo is not falling, gravity is still pulling the yo-yo towards Earth (making it arrow 1). Other forces are acting to offset this force. Arrow 2 indicates a force that would take the yoyo in a straight path, this force is inertia. All objects in motion will travel in a straight line unless an outside force acts upon it. If you have trouble visualizing this, just imagine what will happen to the yo-yo if the string breaks. Arrow 3 is the centripetal force being provided by the string, this is the force that creates the circular motion. Although there is such as thing a centrifugal force the term itself is usually mis-used in replace of centripetal force. Centrifugal force is a complicated subject that has to invovle multiple objects, each with their own inertia and that are acting upon each other.

107. **A grooved wheel turned by a cord or a chain is what kind of simple machine?**
   *(Easy) (Skill 5.6)*

a.   Lever
b.   Inclined Plane
c.   Pulley
d.   Wheel and Axle


**Answer:  c.  Pulley**

A lever is a stick or bar used to pull or pry something. An inclined plane is a ramp. A wheel and axle are a combination of a shaft with a wheel that revolves around it. The answer is (c) a pulley.


108. **Work done divided by the amount of time it took to do it is _____.**
   *(Easy) (Skill 5.7)*

a.   energy
b.   heat
c.   power
d.   efficiency


**Answer:  c.  power**

Power is the work done divided by the amount of time that it took to do it. (Power = Work/Time)

109. **You have four pulley set-ups (in order to solve the problem you don't need the number and size of the pulleys), each with a weight of 1 Newton attched at one end. Based on the energy used to lift the mass and how far the mass was lifted, which of the systems was the most efficient?**
*(Rigorous) (Skill 5.7)*

a. 3 Joules lifted the mass 2 meters
b. 10 Joules lifted the mass 8 meters
c. 4 Joules lifted the mass 3.6 meters
d. 7.5 Joules lifted the mass 6 meters

**Answer: c. 4 Joules lifted the mass 3.6 meters**

Percent efficiency is amount of (useful energy produced / energy used) *100). A joule is equal to the amount of energy required to move an object with a force of 1 Newton a distance of 1 meter. So, the useful energy produced is calculated from multipling the height lifted by the 1 Newton to get how many useful joules were produced, after that the rest is straight arithmetic.
Answer A: (2 m * 1 N / 3 J) *100 = 66.67%
Answer B: (8 m * 1 N / 10 J) *100 = 80%
Answer C: (3.6 m * 1 N / 4 J) *100 = 90%
Answer d: (6 m * 1 N / 7.5 J) *100 = 80%

110. **Sound can be transmitted in all of the following except _____ .**
*(Easy) (Skill 5.8)*

a. air
b. water
c. a diamond
d. a vacuum

**Answer: d. a vacuum**

Sound, a longitudinal wave, is transmitted by vibrations of molecules. Therefore, it can be transmitted through any gas, liquid, or solid. However, it cannot be transmitted through a vacuum, because there are no particles present to vibrate and bump into their adjacent particles to transmit the waves. This is consistent only with answer (d). (It is interesting also to note that sound is actually faster in solids and liquids than in air.)

111.    **Sonar works by _____.**
        *(Easy) (Skill 5.10)*

a.      timing how long it takes sound to reach a certain speed
b.      bouncing sound waves between two metal plates
c.      bouncing sound waves off an underwater object and timing how long it takes for the sound to return
d.      evaluating the motion and amplitude of sound

**Answer:  c.  bouncing sound waves off an object and timing how long it takes for the sound to return**

Sonar is used to measure distances. Sound waves are sent out, and the time is measured for the sound to hit an obstacle and bounce back. By using the known speed of sound, observers (or machines) can calculate the distance to the obstacle. This is consistent only with answer (c).

112.    **As a train approaches, the whistle sounds _____.**
        *(Rigorous) (Skill 5.10)*

a.      higher, because it has a higher apparent frequency
b.      lower, because it has a lower apparent frequency
c.      higher, because it has a lower apparent frequency
d.      lower, because it has a higher apparent frequency

**Answer:  a.  higher, because it has a higher apparent frequency**

By the Doppler effect, when a source of sound is moving toward an observer, the wave fronts are released closer together, i.e. with a greater apparent frequency. Higher frequency sounds are higher in pitch. This is consistent only with answer (a).

113.    **The speed of light is different in different materials. This is responsible for _____ .**
        *(Average Rigor) (Skill 5.11)*

a.      interference
b.      refraction
c.      reflection
d.      relativity


**Answer:  b.  refraction**

Refraction (b) is the bending of light because it hits a material at an angle wherein it has a different speed. (This is analogous to a cart rolling on a smooth road.  If it hits a rough patch at an angle, the wheel on the rough patch slows down first, leading to a change in direction.) Interference (a) is when light waves interfere with each other to form brighter or dimmer patterns; reflection (c) is when light bounces off a surface; relativity (d) is a general topic related to light speed and its implications, but not specifically indicated here. Therefore, the answer is (b).


114.    **Cameras use what kind of lens to produce an image on film?**
        *(Average Rigor) (Skill 5.12)*

a.      Concave
b.      Convex
c.      Convergent
d.      Polarized


**Answer:  b.  Convex**

A polarized lens is one that is most frequently used in sunglasses, because it only allows light through it if the waves are in the right orientation. Convergent is not a term used to describe lenses. A concave les would creat an image like a concave lens, however the image created would be behind the film in most cameras. A convex lens creates an image closer to the lens thus the film and lens can be eassily contained within one device.

115. **When does a converging lens produce a real image?**
*(Rigorous) (Skill 5.12)*

a.  Always
b.  Never
c.  When the object is within one focal length of the lens.
d.  When the object is further than one focal length from the lens.


**Answer:  d.  When the object is further than one focal length from the lens.**

A converging lens produces a real image whenever the object is far enough from the lens (outside one focal length) so that the rays of light from the object can hit the lens and be focused into a real image on the other side of the lens.  When the object is closer than one focal length from the lens, rays of light do not converge on the other side; they diverge. This means that only a virtual image can be formed, i.e. the theoretical place where those diverging rays would have converged if they had originated behind the object. Thus, the correct answer is (d).


116. **Which of the following is not a characteristic of all electrically charged objects?**
*(Average Rigor) (Skill 5.14)*

a.  Opposites attract.
b.  Like repels like.
c.  Charge is conserved.
d.  A magnetic charge develops.


**Answer:  d.  A magnetic charge develops.**

All electrically charged objects share the following characteristics: like charges repel one another, opposite charges attract one another, and charge is conserved. While magnetic charges develop in some electrically charged objects, this does not occur in all electrically charged objects. The answer is (d).

117. **In Ohm's Law (I=V/R), the V represents _____.**
*(Average Rigor) (Skill 5.15)*

a. current
b. amperes
c. potential difference
d. resistance

**Answer:  c.  potential difference**

In Ohm's Law, I stands for current, which is measured in amperes. R stands for resistance, and V stands for potential difference. The answer is (c).

118. **A 10 ohm resistor and a 50 ohm resistor are connected in parallel. If the current in the 10 ohm resistor is 5 amperes, the current (in amperes) running through the 50 ohm resistor is _____.**
*(Average Rigor) (Skill 5.16)*

a. 1
b. 50
c. 250
d. 6

**Answer:  a.  1**

To answer this question, use Ohm's Law, which relates voltage to current and resistance: V = IR where V is voltage; I is current; R is resistance. We also use the fact that in a parallel circuit, the voltage is the same across the branches. Because we are given that in one branch, the current is 5 amperes and the resistance is 10 ohms, we deduce that the voltage in this circuit is their product, 50 volts (from V = IR). We then use V = IR again, this time to find I in the second branch. Because V is 50 volts, and R is 50 ohm, we calculate that I has to be 1 ampere. This is consistent only with answer (a).

119. **A light bulb is connected in series with a rotating coil within a magnetic field. The brightness of the light may be increased by any of the following except _____.**
**(Rigorous) (Skill 5.16)**

a.  rotating the coil more rapidly
b.  using more loops in the coil
c.  using a different color wire for the coil
d.  using a stronger magnetic field

**Answer:  c.  using a different color wire for the coil**

To answer this question, recall that the rotating coil in a magnetic field generates electric current, by Faraday's Law. Faraday's Law states that the amount of emf generated is proportional to the rate of change of magnetic flux through the loop. This increases if the coil is rotated more rapidly (a), if there are more loops (b), or if the magnetic field is stronger (d). Thus, the only answer to this question is (c).

120. **Which component(s) of an atom is most responsible for the development of a magnetic field in an object?**
**(Average Rigor) (Skill 5.17)**

a.  Electrons
b.  Protons
c.  Neutrons
d.  Electrons and Protons

**Answer:  a.  Electrons**

In most objects that can hold a magnetic field the electrons are able to move fairly freely throughout the material (see metallic bonds). This allows electrons spinning in opposite directions to segregate, and it is the segregation that creates that magnetic field. In materials where the electrons are paired in bonding (covalent and ionic bonding for example) the pair usually consists of an electron spinning clockwise and the other spinning counterclockwise. Thus the pair balances each other making it difficult to develop a magnetic field in these materials.

121.    Identify which of the answers has correctly paired the terms with
        their definitions?
        *(Rigorous) (Skill 5.17)*

        I. Amperes          1. Electrical potential
        II. Volts           2. Electrical resistance
        III. Ohms           3. Energy flow
        IV. Watts           4. Electric current

a.      I:1, II:3, III:4, IV:2
b.      I:3, II:1, III:2, IV:4
c.      I:4, II:1, III:2, IV:3
d.      I:3, II:4, III:2, IV:3


**Answer: c. I:4, II:1, III:2, IV:3**

Electrical quantities are most often measured as amperes (electric current), watts
(energy flow), volts (electrical potential), and ohms (resistance). The term
electrical quantity has fallen out of favor among scientists and is now more often
referred to as "charge."


122.    Which of the following is not a way to make an electromagnet more
        powerful?
        *(Rigorous) (Skill 5.17)*

a.      Make more coils.
b.      Put an iron core (nail) inside the coil.
c.      Use more battery power.
d.      Make the coils tighter.


**Answer: d. Make the coils tighter.**

Whereas adding coils of conductive material in essence makes the magnet
bigger, thus leading to a potentially greater magnetic field.Tightening the coils
does not add any additional material and thus doesn't change the level of charge
that can be generated. More battery power means a larger electrical charge
traveling through the coils and this leads to a greater magnetic field. Adding an
iron core allows for the iron to be magnetized along with the coils and thus
generate a greater magnetic field.

123.  Hoover Dam is perhaps the most famous hydroeletric dam in North America. Which on of the follwing best describes how hydroelectric dams generate their power?
      *(Rigorous) (Skill 5.18)*

a.    Gravity imparts kinetic energy onto the falling water, which acts as a mechanical force turning the generator turbines. The turbines contain a coil of wire, and as the turbine spins it spins the coil of wire. This generates an electrical current in the wire that is then sent out to the power grid.

b.    Gravity imparts kinetic energy onto the falling water, which acts as a mechanical force turning the generator turbines. When the turbines spin they spin a series of electromagnets inside a coil of copper wire. This generates an electrical current in the wire that is then sent out to the power grid.

c.    Gravity imparts potential energy onto the falling water, which acts as a mechanical force turning the generator turbines. When the turbines spin they spin a series of electromagnets inside a coil of copper wire. This generates an electrical current in the wire that is then sent out to the power grid.

d.    Gravity imparts kinetic energy onto the falling water, which acts as a mechanical force turning the generator turbines. When the turbines spin they spin a series of permanent magnets inside a coil of copper wire. This generates an electrical current in the wire that is then sent out to the power grid.

**Answer:  b.  Gravity imparts kinetic energy onto the falling water, which acts as a mechanical force turning the generator turbines.**

When the turbines spin, they spin a series of electromagnets inside a coil of copper wire. This generates an electrical current in the wire that is then sent out to the power grid.

Most electric generators work in a process that reverses the process that is used in electric motors.  In a motor, an electromagnet spins in response to the electric current traveling through the coils around it thus creating the mechnical force that drives the motor. A generator just needs a source of mechanical energy to reverse the process and create an electric current.

124. **What is the main obstacle to using nuclear fusion for obtaining electricity?**
     *(Average Rigor) (Skill 5.19)*

a. Nuclear fusion produces much more pollution than nuclear fission.
b. There is no obstacle; most power plants us nuclear fusion today.
c. Nuclear fusion requires very high temperature and activation energy.
d. The fuel for nuclear fusion is extremely expensive.

**Answer: c. Nuclear fusion requires very high temperature and activation energy.**

Nuclear fission is the usual process for power generation in nuclear power plants. This is carried out by splitting nuclei to release energy. The sun's energy is generated by nuclear fusion, i.e. combination of smaller nuclei into a larger nucleus. Fusion creates much less radioactive waste, but it requires extremely high temperature and activation energy, so it is not yet feasible for electricity generation. Therefore, the answer is (c).

125. **In a fission reactor, "heavy water" is used to _____ .**
     *(Rigorous) (Skill 5.19)*

a. terminate fission reactions
b. slow down neutrons and moderate reactions
c. rehydrate the chemicals
d. initiate a chain reaction

**Answer: b. slow down neutrons and moderate reactions**

"Heavy water" is used in a nuclear [fission] reactor to slow down neutrons, controlling and moderating the nuclear reactions. It does not terminate the reaction, and it does not initiate the reaction. Also, although the reactor takes advantage of water's other properties (e.g. high specific heat for cooling), the water does not "rehydrate" the chemicals. Therefore, the answer is (b).

CPSIA information can be obtained
at www.ICGtesting.com
Printed in the USA
BVHW011500300419
546942BV00011B/405/P

9 781642 390582